CONTENTS

Introduction 7

Chapter 1. STEM Basics   9

What Is Science? 10

Fields of Science 11

The Scientific Method 14

ACTIVITY: The Scientific Method in Action 18

ACTIVITY: Science Fiction or Science Fact? 20

Chapter 2. Engineering   23

ACTIVITY: Building a Motor 24

ACTIVITY: Building a Truss 28

ACTIVITY: Building a Bridge 33

ACTIVITY: Building a Circuit 37

ACTIVITY: Insulator versus Conductor 41

ACTIVITY: Electricity and Magnetism: The Two Sisters 47

ACTIVITY: Balloon-Powered Car 52

ACTIVITY: Powering a Boat with Soap 55

ACTIVITY: Mousetrap Car Race 58

ACTIVITY: Water Rocket Launch 64

ACTIVITY: Mini Pyramids—Many Triangles 66

Chapter 3. Physics and Astronomy   69

ACTIVITY: Racing Juice Cans 70

ACTIVITY: Exploring Newton's Third Law 73

ACTIVITY: The Velocity of Bowling Balls 76

ACTIVITY: Static Electricity 79

ACTIVITY: Magnetizing (and Demagnetizing) a Sewing Needle . . . 84

ACTIVITY: What Are Magnets Made Of? 87

ACTIVITY: Keeping a Moon-Phase Journal 90

ACTIVITY: Moon Navigation 93

ACTIVITY: The Easiest Constellations to Recognize 100

Chapter 4. Other Earth Sciences   103

ACTIVITY: North versus South Pole 104

ACTIVITY: Pressure, Temperature, and the Weather 110

ACTIVITY: Why Do Some Things Float? 113

ACTIVITY: Balloons, Spoons, and Density 116

ACTIVITY: The Physics of Floating Feathers 120

ACTIVITY: What's in Soil? 125

Chapter 5. Chemistry   129

ACTIVITY: How Batteries Work 130

ACTIVITY: Alkaline or Acidic? 135

ACTIVITY: The pH of Foods 139

ACTIVITY: Separating Salt from Water. 143

ACTIVITY: Ice versus Dry Ice 146

Chapter 6. Biology   149

ACTIVITY: How Plants Make Food: Photosynthesis 150

ACTIVITY: Deciduous versus Evergreen Trees. 154

ACTIVITY: Fermentation: Making Sourdough Starter 159

ACTIVITY: Potato, Carrot, and Cell Osmosis 163

ACTIVITY: Dominant versus Recessive Traits 168

Chapter 7. Mathematics and Computer Science   171

ACTIVITY: Designing Wallpaper Using Percentages. 172

ACTIVITY: Tic-Tac-Toe Math Review. 175

ACTIVITY: Algebra Dice 179

ACTIVITY: Calculating the Circumference of a Pie,
Bike Wheel, Car Tire, Etc. 183

ACTIVITY: The Cartesian Treasure Map 186

ACTIVITY: The Geometry Scavenger Hunt 190

ACTIVITY: Mean, Median, and Mode 193

ACTIVITY: Pies and Bars. 199

ACTIVITY: Learning Probability with Cards and Dice 207

ACTIVITY: The Birthday Problem 216

ACTIVITY: How Many Zeros Are in a Quadrillion? 218

ACTIVITY: Money's Value over Time. 222

Chapter 8. Getting a Head Start in STEM 227

STEM Camps and Enrichment Classes 228

Online STEM Classes 231

Other Online Learning Resources 233

Job Shadowing. 236

Appendix A. STEM Career Websites for Kids 241

Appendix B. Bibliography 244

Index. 253

INTRODUCTION

Short for science, technology, engineering, and mathematics, STEM represents much more than a collection of school subjects or classes. It's an exciting world that goes well beyond the walls of a classroom and into the world around us. STEM answers countless questions kids (and adults!) ask every day: How exactly does a bridge stay up? What do meteorologists mean by "high pressure" and "low pressure"? Why are there so few people with red hair? What's the probability that someone else has the same birthday as you?

Figuring out the answers to these questions doesn't have to be boring, intimidating, or done by a trained scientist. You can unearth them with your whole family, in your own home, with materials you have on hand.

Kids are naturally curious about the world around them—nurture that curiosity with fun, engaging activities that teach as they entertain. Your daughter might discover that she has a real knack for statistics—maybe she'd like her school's math club. Your son might realize he loves all things plants, and start volunteering at the community garden. These interests could even spawn a successful career well down the road.

According to the Bureau of Labor Statistics of the U.S. Department of Labor, unemployment rates are lower and average wages are higher in STEM fields than in non-STEM fields. Job market analytics company Burning Glass Technologies found that entry-level jobs in STEM pay roughly 28 percent more on average than entry-level jobs in other fields. Despite these healthy job prospects in STEM, many young people choose other paths. Some likely steer clear of STEM because the subjects are difficult. One way you can help your kids face challenging coursework is by providing opportunities for learning outside the classroom—such as the activities in this book.

Even if your child doesn't choose a career in STEM later in life, the activities in this book will help him or her develop the kind of critical thinking skills necessary in a wide variety of classes, internships, and jobs: A nonprofit fundraiser needs to master how to calculate compound interest; a chef should know how certain ingredients interact on a chemical level; and it's essential for a soccer coach to understand Newton's three laws of motion.

What's Your STEM? offers more than fifty learning activities designed to introduce young learners to a wide variety of STEM fields. You'll want to do many of the activities with your child, to guide and oversee the process. Depending on the age and aptitude of your child, she may enjoy exploring some of the activities on her own. In addition to the hands-on activities, *What's Your STEM?* describes a variety of STEM careers your child might like to hear about—from aerospace engineer to web developer.

Use these activities to take STEM beyond the classroom, out from under its educational acronym, and into your home. Build your child's confidence, fuel passions, and spark interests. Make STEM concepts familiar, achievable, exciting—and above all, fun.

CHAPTER 1
STEM BASICS

If you don't work in a STEM field, you might need a refresher on some fundamental concepts before you start working with your child on the activities in the book. This chapter offers a basic introduction to the various fields in the industry, and includes a hands-on learning activity designed to help you explore the scientific method.

What Is Science?

When you hear the word "science," a number of images probably come immediately into your mind. You might think of a laboratory featuring beakers and Bunsen burners, or a scientist in a white lab coat looking through a microscope, or a tweed-coated professor peering at the stars through a telescope. Perhaps the word conjures up images of the periodic table, or high-school biology students dissecting a frog. Science certainly includes images like those, but it's a broader concept than many people realize.

Science is a process for discovering knowledge or uncovering general truths based on observation and experimentation. Science also refers to the body of knowledge that results from that process. You can think of science as a process of discovery, along with all the discoveries that are made along the way and the application of those discoveries.

STEM Words to Know

serendipity

Not all scientific discoveries arrive through experimentation—some have come more or less by accident. A happy accident like that is called *serendipity*, and there are many examples of it occurring in science throughout the years. Alexander Fleming, a Scottish scientist, left a petri dish open by mistake and it became contaminated by a bacteria-killing mold. That "accident" marked the discovery of penicillin. While testing radar equipment for the Raytheon company, a worker noticed that a candy bar had melted in his pocket, leading to the development of the microwave oven. Safety glass came about when a lab worker forgot to wash out a glass beaker and the plastic that it had contained coated the inside of the beaker.

One of the most basic distinctions is to divide scientific work into basic science and applied science. *Basic science* involves the discovery of new knowledge or fundamental principles. *Applied science* involves utilizing already existing knowledge for some purpose. The discovery of x-rays would be considered basic science. The use of x-rays to examine fractured bones is applied science. All fields of science have basic aspects and applied aspects.

Fields of Science

Science is divided into a number of scientific disciplines or fields. The major scientific fields are then further divided into subfields. Here are some of the most common STEM fields.

Science Teacher

Anyone who decides to become a teacher must have patience, dedication, and a real desire to help others. Teachers of STEM subjects need extra patience and skill because so many students have a fear of math and science.

Public school teachers need a license or certification in the state they teach in and in the subject they teach. They need a passing score on a set of exams called the Praxis exams. The demand for teachers varies by state and city, and also by subject area. The overall demand for science and math teachers is greater than the demand for teachers of other subjects. Ask current teachers for any advice they have to offer about this important and rewarding career.

Life Sciences

The life sciences are those fields involving the study of living organisms, including biology and its subfields. Some of the life science subfields are biochemistry, anatomy, genetics, botany, horticulture, zoology, microbiology, food science, and environmental health. Medicine is also part of the life sciences.

Physical Sciences and Mathematics

The physical sciences focus on the study of nonliving matter and energy. The physical sciences include all the subfields of physics, chemistry, earth science, and atmospheric sciences.

Mathematics also has a number of divisions and subfields. The computer sciences are also grouped under this broad category.

PHYSICS

Physics involves the study of matter and energy. Some of the subfields in physics are fluid dynamics, optics, nuclear physics, quantum physics, astronomy, and astrophysics. Physics principles are employed in many other science and technology fields.

CHEMISTRY

Chemistry focuses on the composition and properties of substances, as well as the interactions among substances. Subfields are organic chemistry, analytical chemistry, and biochemistry.

STEM Words to Know

nanotechnology

An emerging area of engineering is nanoscience, which involves the creation of nanotechnology. The National Nanotechnology Initiative claims that, "[n]anoscience and nanotechnology are the study and application of extremely small things and can be used across all the other science fields." Just to give you an idea of how small the nanoscale is, there are 25,400,000 nanometers in an inch.

EARTH SCIENCE

Earth science includes all the subfields related to the study of the earth's makeup. Geology, paleontology, soil science, volcanology, and seismology are among the earth science subfields.

OCEANOGRAPHY, ATMOSPHERIC SCIENCES, AND METEOROLOGY

Oceanography is the study of oceans and marine life. The atmospheric sciences and meteorology involve the study of the weather and climate and their impact on the earth.

MATHEMATICS, APPLIED MATHEMATICS, AND STATISTICS

The field of mathematics involves the study of numbers, equations, shapes, and their relationships. Some of its subfields are algebra, number theory, and set theory. Applied mathematics focuses on the use of math concepts in other fields, such as engineering and business. Control theory and dynamic systems are examples of subfields in applied mathematics. Statistics involves gathering, analyzing, and presenting data.

COMPUTER SCIENCES

Computer sciences deal with computers and their practical applications. Subfields include databases/information systems, programming languages, and artificial intelligence/robotics.

Science Writer

Science writers write articles and blog posts for magazines, newspapers, and websites. Some science writers are so intrigued by their subjects that they write full-length books. Science writers don't have to be scientists; many train as journalists and then later decide to focus their attention on science. Some science writers specialize in one or a few popular niche areas, such as space travel, artificial intelligence, or biotechnology.

Those interested in a career in science writing should, of course, regularly read science articles and books, both in their specialty area and beyond. Reading the work of other science writers helps the aspiring writer learn the style of writing that readers expect and discover which science topics people find most interesting.

Engineering

Engineering involves the practical application of science and math for the purpose of designing and building physical structures and machines, or otherwise managing resources. Some engineering fields are mechanical engineering, civil engineering, aerospace engineering, industrial engineering, nuclear engineering, and electrical engineering.

Social and Behavioral Sciences

The social and behavioral sciences are those that examine how humans behave, either as individuals or as part of a group. Some examples of social and behavioral sciences are anthropology, psychology, economics, sociology, and political science.

The Scientific Method

Early humans developed many theories about why the world works the way it does. There were fanciful explanations for various natural phenomena, many of them involving unseen forces, such as gods and goddesses. Lightning storms, earthquakes, even the rising and setting of the sun all had explanations based on the actions of various deities. Those explanations may have made for entertaining stories, but there was nothing scientific about them.

The scientist Ibn al-Haytham, who lived during the tenth and eleventh centuries, made one of the earliest statements about the scientific method in his book *Doubts Concerning Ptolemy*.

The seeker after the truth is not one who studies the writings of the ancients and, following his natural disposition, puts his trust in them, but rather the one who suspects his faith in them and questions what he gathers from them, the one who submits to argument and demonstration and not to the sayings of a human being whose nature is fraught with all kinds of imperfection and deficiency.

Ibn al-Haytham's statement captures the basic idea behind scientific inquiry, or what has come to be known as *the scientific method*. The theories and principles that are widely accepted in each of the various sciences were not accepted immediately. Each was subjected to lots of analysis and verification. In some cases, the theories were only partially correct and had to be corrected or completed by later scientists. The scientific method has been employed in the discovery and refinement of many important findings in science.

Steps of the Scientific Method

The particular application of the scientific method may differ some from field to field, but the basic process is the same in all sciences. The scientific method can be broken down into a few fundamental steps.

STEP 1: ASK A GENERAL QUESTION

Scientific inquiry begins with a researcher asking a general question. For example, suppose you begin to wonder about the new chemical factory that was just built in your neighborhood close to your favorite fishing stream. In particular, you wonder if the factory will harm the stream in some way. That's your general question: Will the new chemical factory affect the local stream?

STEP 2: GATHER BACKGROUND INFORMATION

As a researcher, you always want to know what other research has been done on your subject. Most researchers read a lot about their subject, particularly any work that was published recently. Researchers also need a good understanding of the fundamental science, or the widely accepted principles, relating to their research. To analyze the question about the chemical factory and the stream, it would be good for the researcher to have a background in environmental science or some related field.

STEP 3: FORM A HYPOTHESIS

A *hypothesis* is a proposition about the cause or nature of something. For it to be used as part of the scientific method, a hypothesis must be testable. For example, a man who lost his car keys could form the hypothesis that his keys were stolen by leprechauns. Since there's no obvious way to scientifically test whether or not leprechauns stole his car keys, the man's hypothesis can't be explored with the scientific method. The man's hypothesis would be considered highly *nonscientific* in light of the fact that science doesn't generally acknowledge the existence of leprechauns!

You also can't test hypotheses that are statements of value judgment. For example, the statement "people who drive yellow cars have poor taste" is not a testable hypothesis, because good taste and poor taste are all in the eye of the beholder.

Following are some examples of testable hypotheses.

- Cigarette smokers are more likely to develop lung cancer than nonsmokers
- Married people tend to live longer than unmarried people, all else being equal
- Kids tend to become hyperactive when they eat too much sugar
- Plants grow faster when exposed to classical music
- People who take regular vacations have lower stress levels than people who rarely vacation

In your research about the factory's effects on the stream, you could start with a hypothesis such as "Most factories emit pollutants that are dangerous to the environment and the health of living things."

STEP 4: TEST THE HYPOTHESIS

After stating your hypothesis, it's time to look for a way to test it. Some tests of hypotheses are easy to conduct; others take a lot of time and resources. For example, you could state the following hypothesis: "A 1-pound brick dropped from 5 feet will reach the ground in less than 2 seconds." Such a hypothesis would be easy to test by performing a simple experiment. You could simply drop the brick from 5 feet and time how long it takes the brick to reach the ground. Usually scientists will want to repeat an experiment a number of times to verify the results. If you dropped the brick several times in a row and each time it reached the ground in less than 2 seconds, you could be pretty certain of your results.

Experiments are used to gather data about the hypothesis being tested. Each time you drop the brick, you record the length of time it takes the brick to reach the ground. Each time you repeat the experiment and record the result, you're making an *observation*. The data or observations you're recording—generated by repeated trials of your experiment—are what you'll analyze to determine whether your stated hypothesis is true. But experiments are not the only method used to gather data. Social scientists often use surveys to collect information. For example, if you wanted to find out how people feel about a particular political candidate, you could conduct a survey, asking people their opinion of the candidate.

Sometimes scientists use data that already exists. For example, if you needed to know the population of the United States in order to test your hypothesis, you wouldn't be required to count the number of people living in the country. The U.S. Census Bureau gathers population data for the nation, and anyone can use the data. When you utilize data that's been gathered by someone else, it's known as *secondary data*. (If you did count the citizens yourself, you would be gathering *primary data*.)

For your factory-effects-on-stream research, you could do searches online (such as "factory pollutants" and "industrial water pollution") to find websites that have useful secondary data.

STEP 5: ANALYZE THE DATA AND MAKE A CONCLUSION

The final step in the scientific process is to analyze the data you've gathered and make a conclusion about your stated hypothesis. If your hypothesis turns out false, you might repeat your procedure to be sure you didn't make any errors in conducting the experiment or recording the data. Even if you prove your hypothesis, it's a good idea to review your procedure to be sure it's error-free.

After reaching a conclusion about your hypothesis, you'll want to communicate your results, either in the form of an oral presentation or a written report. For as long as the scientific method has existed, scientists have communicated the results of their work so that others could build upon it and advance the sciences.

THE SCIENTIFIC METHOD IN ACTION

This famous experiment that kids have been doing for decades requires only an eyedropper and a few coins. The basic purpose of the experiment is to introduce the scientific method.

MATERIALS NEEDED:
- A penny, a dime, and a quarter
- A clean eyedropper
- Water
- 2 other kinds of safe liquids
- A pencil or pen
- A table for recording observations (see following example)

There are several ways to approach this activity. One is to begin with the smallest coin, a dime, and an eyedropper filled with tap water. Invite your child to squeeze one drop of water onto the dime and then observe how the water behaves. After your child has observed the water for a moment, ask her to make a prediction about how many drops of water will fit on the dime before the water spills off the coin's edge. Help her craft her prediction into a testable statement of hypothesis before she proceeds with the experiment.

After your child records the number of water drops the dime held, ask her to make a conclusion about whether her hypothesis was correct or not. Then ask her to make a prediction (i.e., state a hypothesis) about the number of water drops a penny will hold. After she has completed her experiment and made her conclusion about the penny, have her repeat the process with a quarter.

If your child is particularly inquisitive, invite her to repeat the entire process (penny, dime, and quarter) using two other safe liquids. Some possible choices include milk, soda, and cooking oil. Be sure to clean the coins and the eyedropper after each round. For the rounds involving other liquids, encourage your child to form statements of hypothesis that include some comparison to water (e.g., fewer drops of milk will fit on the penny than drops of water).

RECORD YOUR RESULTS: THE COIN AND LIQUID EXPERIMENT			
	Number of Drops		
Liquid	Dime	Penny	Quarter
Water			
Milk			
Soda			
Oil			
Other Liquid			

The actual science underlying the eyedropper activity is somewhat advanced. If your child is deeply interested in science, encourage her to seek out the scientific explanation online or in the library. The point of the activity is to introduce her to the basic steps of the scientific method, and expose her to some basic STEM vocabulary.

Although it has its limitations, the scientific method has endured for centuries thanks to the millions of insights and advances it has yielded. Without the advent of the scientific method, the pursuit of scientific knowledge wouldn't have followed the trajectory it has, and human life wouldn't be the same as we know it today.

ACTIVITY:
SCIENCE FICTION OR SCIENCE FACT?

Science Fiction or Science Fact is a game you can play anywhere, and it's a game that constantly changes. The basic premise of the game isn't complicated. One person makes a statement relating to some scientific development, and then another person determines whether that statement is science fiction or science fact. The game constantly changes because the frontiers of science are always advancing.

Some ideas that you can use for the game are listed here. You can also find ideas by reading magazines such as *Scientific American* or *Popular Science* or looking at their websites. These statements represent science facts that probably sound like a lot like science fiction.

SCIENCE FACTS THAT SOUND LIKE SCIENCE FICTION:

- Robots have been developed that climb walls like insects
- Medical researchers have succeeded in creating artificial blood
- An invisibility device has been developed that uses lenses to cloak a small object
- Scientists have modified silkworms to create silk that's stronger than steel
- Some Earth organisms have survived in space without a spacesuit or other protection
- Astronomers have discovered that planets can exist in systems with multiple suns
- The FDA has approved a bionic eye that enables blind people to see
- Scientists have teleported individual atoms from one location to another

For statements of pure science fiction, you can be as creative as you want. Just to get your juices flowing, a few statements of pure science fiction are listed here.

STATEMENTS OF PURE SCIENCE FICTION (FOR THE TIME BEING):

- Scientists have cloned dinosaurs from fossils
- Astronomers have spotted alien life forms on Europa, one of Jupiter's moons
- A mineral was discovered that, when digested, can completely stop the aging process
- A helicopter was invented that can fly underwater
- Japan's space agency has developed an escalator that carries humans to space
- Bioengineers dug up a corpse and brought it back to life using nanotechnology
- A monkey was genetically modified to give birth to a human baby
- Archaeologists have discovered evidence that the Greek god Zeus once really existed
- Technology exists that can send astronauts to neighboring star systems
- Dog breeders have bred a special new breed of dog that doesn't eat or go to the bathroom

In some cases, there have been hoaxes in which science fiction has been portrayed as science fact. For example, a statement about British scientists cloning dinosaurs from fossils was once released, but it was proved to be a prank. As you search for additional material for the game, be sure to choose your sources carefully.

CHAPTER 2

ENGINEERING

In the modern world, people are surrounded by all kinds of structures built by engineers and architects. Some of those structures are stationary, such as buildings, bridges, and towers. Other structures have parts that move or rotate, such as mechanical structures that use motors.

This chapter explores the design ideas and the thought processes behind many types of engineering projects. The chapter also includes descriptions of some of the engineering jobs that are essential in an industrial society.

BUILDING A MOTOR

A motor is a machine that can make objects rotate. An electric motor's input is electricity and its output is mechanical movement in the form of rotation. That may sound a little complicated, but you're about to find out how simple it is to make a homemade electric motor. We'll focus on building a direct current (or DC) motor that uses batteries. Most of the materials needed can be purchased from a hardware store and a craft store.

MATERIALS NEEDED:
- 20" length of enameled copper wire, 26 gauge (AWG)
- 2 connecting wires with alligator clip ends
- 6-volt battery
- Cylindrical neodymium magnet ½" in diameter and ½" in height
- 2 large safety pins
- Smooth Styrofoam disk
- Dowel with ½" diameter and 4" in length
- Sandpaper
- Pliers

PROCEDURE:
1. Assist your child in taking the stretch of copper wire and winding it around the dowel 4–5 times. Once he has 4–5 turns of wire, tell him to remove the dowel and wrap the loose end of the wire around the looped wires twice to make a knot and tighten the loops together, as shown in the following picture. Have him do the same at the other loose end of the copper wire. Make sure the excess straight wire on either end is along a straight line. This will serve as a shaft, about which the motor will rotate.

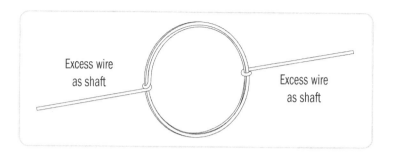

Excess wire as shaft

Excess wire as shaft

2. Use sandpaper to entirely remove the enamel from one end of the straight copper wire. Lay the loop flat on a surface, and use the sandpaper to remove the enamel only from the top face of the other straight wire that's not yet sanded (see the following illustration).

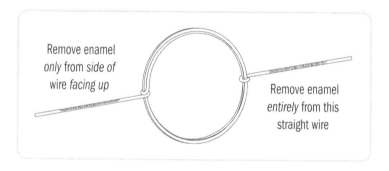

Remove enamel *only* from *side of* wire *facing up*

Remove enamel *entirely* from this straight wire

3. Use a pair of pliers to clip off the fastening end of two safety pins (right).

4. Now have your child push the neodymium magnet halfway into the Styrofoam disk so that it sticks slightly above the Styrofoam surface level. Place the safety pins down on either side of the magnet so that each forms a triangle pointing up. Place the looped copper wire in such a way that its shaft rests inside the holes of the safety pins (see the following illustration). Note: You might need to push the safety pins farther into the Styrofoam in order to bring the looped copper wire very close to the magnet (without touching it).

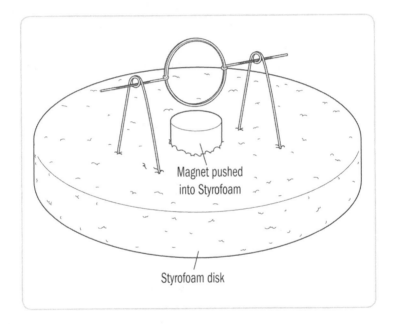

Magnet pushed into Styrofoam

Styrofoam disk

5. Next, ask your child to use an alligator clip wire to connect the base of one safety pin to the positive terminal of the battery, and another alligator clip wire to connect the base of the other safety pin to the negative terminal of the battery (see the following illustration).

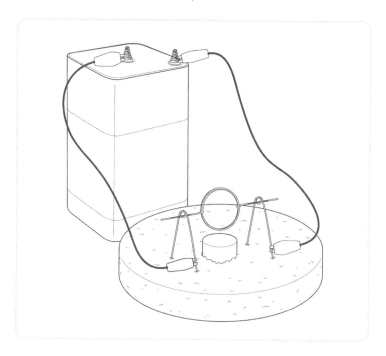

Use your forefinger to give the copper loop a little spin and watch it spin around on its own afterward!

The little motor you created may not power a car—or even a food processor—but it will surely delight the young person who built it!

ACTIVITY:
BUILDING A TRUSS

Trusses are found in virtually every modern building. They're used to provide support for the structure so it can withstand heavy loads. Trusses can be seen in the roofs of large stores, in bridges, and in football stadiums—among countless other places.

What exactly is a truss? What's the simplest way to construct a truss? Who uses trusses and for what purpose? What are trusses made of?

A truss is a two-dimensional structure (a plane) made of straight segments of wood or metal connected together to form triangles. In terms of stability and strength, a triangle can keep its shape under a heavy load better than a square can. In the following diagram, you can see how a load on the triangle is distributed through its sides such that the structure of the triangle holds its shape firmly and doesn't collapse.

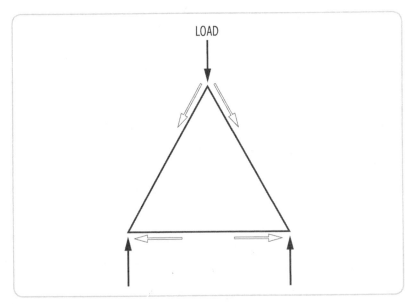

In contrast, when a square structure is loaded, the square will change its shape into a rhombus where its angles are no longer right angles, as shown in the next diagram. Such a structure doesn't hold its shape, and it collapses when loaded.

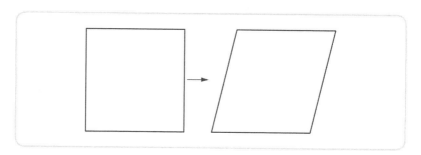

One way a square can be supported so that it doesn't lose its structure is to connect the two opposite corners with a diagonal line, turning the square into two triangles (right). This demonstrates how essential the shape of a triangle is in building stable structures.

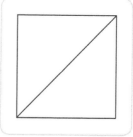

A truss is made of connecting triangles. The simplest such truss can be constructed of two adjacent triangles that have a connecting line on top (below).

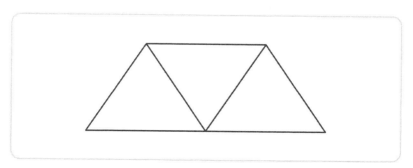

Such a truss is historically known as a Warren truss. The shape of this truss was patented by the British engineer James Warren in 1848. When many of these triangles are connected to form a longer truss, they can be used in building a bridge (below).

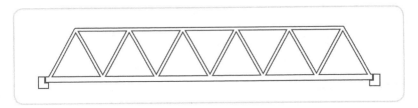

Another example of the support abilities of triangles can be seen in the wings of old propeller biplanes. The wings were stacked on top of one another, supported by trusses.

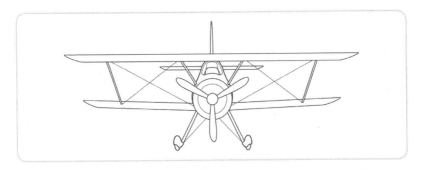

Here's an easy way to construct a truss at home.

MATERIALS NEEDED:
- 15–19 Popsicle sticks
- Glue gun
- Glue sticks (for glue gun)

PROCEDURE:
1. Assist your child in using the glue gun. Ask her to form a triangle by gluing together the ends of 3 Popsicle sticks, as shown in the first diagram on the opposite page.

2. Using the glue gun, have your child attach a fourth Popsicle stick horizontally at the top corner of the triangle, as shown in the second diagram on this page.

3. Next, have your child glue a fifth Popsicle stick diagonally to form the second (upside-down) triangle.

4. Have your child glue a sixth Popsicle stick horizontally on the bottom. Ask her to continue to repeat the steps of adding a diagonal then a horizontal stick each time, until she uses all 15 sticks. If she is excited about making a longer truss, she can use all 19 sticks.

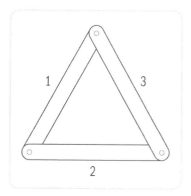

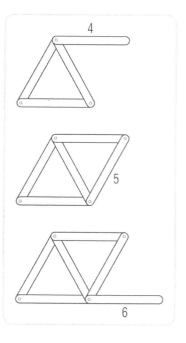

When your child is done gluing all the sticks according to the diagram, ask her what kind of truss she now has. Does it look like a famous truss that is named after someone? Of course, it is a Warren truss, as described earlier.

There are other types of trusses besides the Warren truss. Other known trusses are shown in this next diagram. Try to spot all the triangles in each truss. Some trusses use equilateral triangles, like the Warren truss. Other trusses use right-angle triangles, like the Howe and the Pratt trusses. There's also the K truss, which uses triangles making the shape of the letter K.

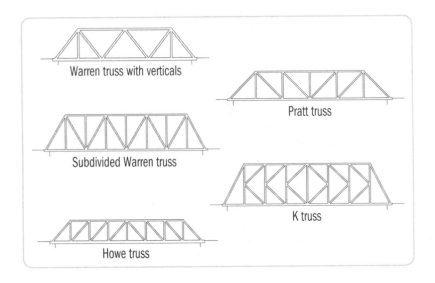

Warren truss with verticals

Pratt truss

Subdivided Warren truss

K truss

Howe truss

There are many other types of trusses, most of which you can see via a simple Internet search.

Civil Engineer

A civil engineer designs and builds construction projects. This includes roads, bridges, dams, buildings, airports, tunnels, railway systems, water supply systems, and wastewater treatment plants. Civil engineers also work on projects such as designing facilities for disposal of hazardous waste and building diversions to control floods and supervising construction projects.

Civil engineers work both indoors and outdoors. They are often found at construction sites supervising and monitoring operations, and solving any problems that may arise at the site. Civil engineers learn a lot about soil mechanics because they have to work with soil directly—for example, when building foundations.

ACTIVITY:

BUILDING A BRIDGE

Seeing a bridge is a common, everyday occurrence for most people. When crossing a river or any waterway, you have to drive on or walk along a bridge. You might even walk along a people bridge constructed between buildings in a large hospital or company complex.

Bridges are often supported by trusses. As discussed in the previous section, a truss is a structure formed of connected segments of triangles, usually made of a material such as steel or wood. A truss is most commonly two-dimensional, meaning flat, like a board. In order to construct a bridge—which is three-dimensional—many trusses are incorporated into the bridge design.

Regardless of the kind of bridge—its style, its purpose, whether it supports people or vehicles—all truss bridges rely on trusses to support their load-carrying structures.

The simplest design for a truss is the Warren truss. Although the design of such a bridge is simple, it still can hold a large load. You can build a simple bridge by constructing two Warren trusses and a walkway. In order to find out how strong your bridge is, you'll need a luggage scale to test how much force your bridge can support.

MATERIALS NEEDED:
- Bag of Popsicle sticks
- Glue gun
- Glue sticks (for glue gun)
- Bag of cable ties
- Scissors
- Digital luggage scale
- 2' length of twisted nylon rope ½" in diameter

PROCEDURE:

1. Assist your child in using the glue gun. Ask him to form a triangle by gluing together the ends of 3 Popsicle sticks, as shown in the diagram to the right.

2. Using the glue gun, have your child attach other Popsicle sticks, one at a time, in the order of the numbering shown in the next diagram. Tell him to add the sticks with care, making sure the top horizontal sticks and the bottom horizontal sticks line up along as straight a line as possible.

3. Ask your child to glue together as many as 19 sticks following the pattern described, until his truss looks like the one in the diagram below.

4. Tell your child to assemble the same shape truss again, using the same number of sticks. He should have two

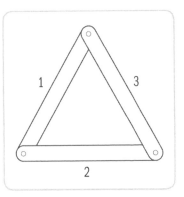

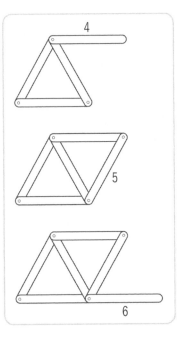

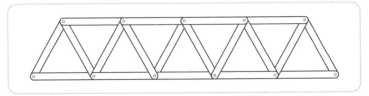

such Warren trusses that will form the sides of his bridge when he finally assembles it.

5. Now it's time for your child to make the bottom walkway of the bridge. Ask him to glue together 4 Popsicle sticks in one long straight line. Have him make two such long lines of sticks.

6. Tell your child to set the two long lines of sticks on the table parallel to each other, so that the distance between the two lines is the length of one Popsicle stick.

7. Ask your child to place more Popsicle sticks perpendicular to the two long lines in such a way that they look like a ladder, and to secure them in place with glue. Lay the perpendicular sticks very close to each other, so that they are about ¼" apart.

8. Now have your child reinforce the bottom walkway with diagonal Popsicle sticks, as shown below. Remind him to secure the additional Popsicle sticks in place with glue.

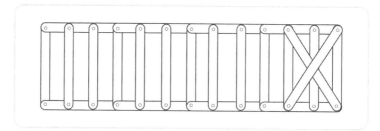

9. Tell your child to place diagonal Popsicle sticks along the entire length of the bottom walkway.

10. It's now time to assemble the bridge. Tell your child to place the Warren trusses he built earlier along either side of the bottom walkway. Let the top lengths of the two trusses touch, like the two sides of a house roof meet to form a triangular shape.

11. Using the cable ties, tie the side of the bottom walkway to the bottom of one truss. Do so at both ends, and every couple

of inches along the length of the truss. Do the same for the other truss. Finally, tie the two top lengths of the trusses together and secure them every couple of inches along the length of the bridge top.

12. Now it's time to test the strength of the bridge Place the ends of the bridge on the edges of two tables situated side by side so that there is only air underneath the bridge. Using the nylon rope, make a vertical loop around the bridge. So you should have two trusses and a walkway. The two trusses connect together on top, forming a triangular shape like the roof of a house, and the walkway in the base of the triangular shape. Hang the luggage scale from it.

13. Using his own strength, have your child pull the luggage scale down and note the reading on the scale. How much downward force can his bridge support?

If your child's bridge can support 50 or 60 pounds of force, then he's constructed a pretty sturdy bridge out of Popsicle sticks, using trusses and triangles.

There have been other famous bridges built to last. Some are supported by pillars on the bottom of the bridge and cantilevers that extend horizontally, such as the Forth Bridge in the east of Scotland, just a little west of the city of Edinburgh. Some bridges are suspension bridges that are hung by suspension cables, such as the famous Golden Gate Bridge. But a bridge, whether it's a suspension bridge or not, wouldn't be nearly as strong without trusses.

BUILDING A CIRCUIT

Electric circuits are everywhere in our lives. When you turn on your desk lamp, it lights up because it's connected to an electric circuit. For the same reason, the burner on your electric stove gets hot and turns red when you switch it on. Your cell phone flashlight comes on and the phone's other normal functions are possible because of the massive electrical circuitry housed within it.

These examples may make it sound as if electric circuits are very complicated, but they don't always have to be. You can build a simple electric circuit out of pretty basic items at home.

MATERIALS NEEDED:

- 5 miniature light bulbs rated 2.5V 0.3A
- 5 miniature bulb holders with circular plastic bases
- 3 size-D batteries
- Electrical tape
- 6 alligator clip wires

PROCEDURE:

1. Using the electrical tape, assist your child in securing the 3 D batteries in a row, end to end. Make sure the positive end (labeled +) of one battery is snuggled tightly against the negative end (labeled –) of the next battery before you secure them with the electrical tape. Now the battery pack is ready.
2. Assist your child in taping one end of an alligator clip wire to one end of the battery pack. Then help her tape another alligator clip wire to the other end of the battery pack.
3. Ask your child to screw each light bulb into the bulb holders so they can be ready for use. Assist her in noticing how each

bulb holder has two metal ears (as shown in the following figure) where alligator clip wires can be attached.

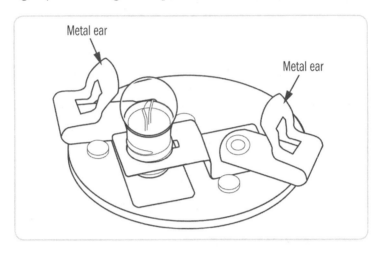

Metal ear

Metal ear

4. Using the wire attached to the positive side of the battery pack, clip the loose end of that wire onto a metal ear of the bulb holder.
5. Now use another alligator clip wire to connect the other metal ear of the bulb holder to a second bulb holder.

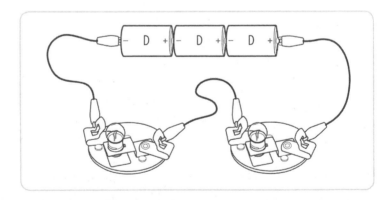

6. Next, connect the loose wire on the negative side of the battery pack to the second bulb holder. What do you observe? Do both light bulbs light up?

7. Now disconnect the wire between the two bulb holders.
8. Ask your child to connect a third light bulb with its holder in between the other two, as shown in the diagram. Notice what happens to the brightness of all bulbs compared to when there were two bulbs.

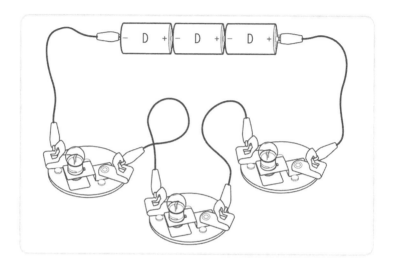

9. Suggest to your child to add yet a fourth bulb in the same fashion she added the third one. What do you observe regarding the brightness of all bulbs compared to when there were three bulbs?
10. Finally, go ahead and add a fifth bulb. What do you observe regarding the brightness of all the bulbs compared to when there were four bulbs?

Did you observe the bulbs getting dimmer and dimmer as you added more bulbs into the circuit?

A connected electric circuit allows electric charges (such as electrons) to move inside the wires in a fashion similar to traffic. Notice how the bulbs allowed you to "see" that traffic in motion. This traffic of electric charges is known as *electric current*. In a way it is like the current in a river, except the river current is moving water. Electric current is moving charges.

What do you think the light bulbs do to that traffic (or current)? Do you think they help the traffic move faster or slower? Do they help that traffic speed up or slow down? (Remember that the bulbs got dimmer as you added more.)

If your child concluded that the bulbs act as obstacles to the electron traffic flow, then she was right on. The light bulbs create resistance to the flow of electrons in the wires, slowing them down. It's similar to having more accidents along the highway that slow down traffic.

The flashlight in your cell phone works in a similar fashion. This is only one example of many other more complicated electric circuits. Even though the circuits can get more complex, they all operate under the same principles with respect to moving electrons.

The Difference Between Electric Circuits and Static Electricity

There are several differences between electric circuits and static electricity. One difference is that electrons *move* inside the wires in electric circuits, but they remain stationary—*not moving*—when static electricity builds up. Also, all parts of an electric circuit must be connected and able to allow electrons to move through, so they must be made of conductors such as metal, while static electricity can only stay put on insulated material, such as plastic. Another important difference is that a power source, like a battery, is needed for an electric circuit, but is not needed to build up static electricity on an object.

The next time you turn on a burner in your stove and watch it get bright red, remember that you're watching electrons in motion inside the stove's electric circuits as those electrons "light up" the burner.

ACTIVITY:

INSULATOR VERSUS CONDUCTOR

There are always warnings against letting a small child stick his finger in an electric socket. The danger of an electric shock is definitely no joke. But what is it about the human body that allows one to be electrically shocked? Is there a way to prevent one from being shocked when touching a live electrical wire?

The property that allows an object to let electricity move through it is called *conductivity*. A *conductor* is an object that allows electricity to move through it—i.e., it conducts electricity. As you might guess, the human body is one example of a conductor. There's a category of objects that do not allow electricity to move through. Those objects are known as *insulators*. Rubber is a good example of an insulator.

Is there a safe way to test which materials are conductors and which are insulators (without being electrically shocked)? Absolutely, there is.

MATERIALS NEEDED:
- 2 miniature light bulbs rated 2.5V 0.3A
- 2 miniature bulb holders with plastic circular bases
- 3 size-D batteries
- Electrical tape
- 4 alligator clip wires
- Sewing needle
- Plastic lid
- Styrofoam peanut
- Pencil lead
- Human fingernail (after cutting your nails)
- Human hair
- Stainless steel pot
- Drinking glass

- Ceramic plate
- Wooden toothpick
- Tap water
- Salt

PROCEDURE:
1. Using the electrical tape, assist your child in securing the 3 D batteries in a row, end to end. Make sure the positive end (labeled +) of one battery is snuggled against the negative end (labeled –) of the next battery.
2. Assist your child in taping one end of an alligator clip wire to one end of the battery pack. Then help her tape another alligator clip wire to the other end of the battery pack.
3. Ask your child to screw each light bulb into the bulb holders so they can be ready for use. Notice how each bulb holder has two metal ears (as shown in the following figure) where alligator clip wires can be attached.

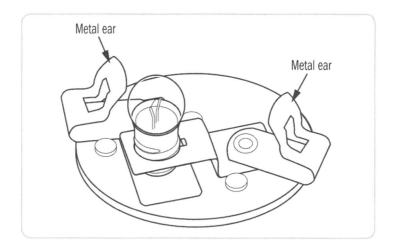

4. Using the wire attached to the positive side of the battery pack, clip the loose end of that wire onto a metal ear of the bulb holder.

5. Next, connect the loose wire on the negative side of the battery pack to the second bulb holder.
6. Now tell your child to use another alligator clip wire to connect to the other metal ear of the bulb holder, leaving that wire loose. Do so for both bulbs, as shown in the following diagram.

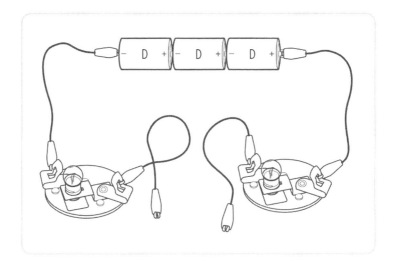

7. Tell your child to connect the two loose wire ends to either side of the sewing needle by clipping them. What happens to the light bulbs? Do the bulbs light up or stay off?
8. Assist your child in organizing the results of her observations by recording them in the second column in the following table.
9. Ask your child to remove the sewing needle, and connect the plastic lid between the two loose wire ends. What happened? Did the bulbs light up? Tell her to record her observation in the table.
10. Ask your child to test each of the materials in the list and record her observation of the light bulbs for each item in the table.

11. If your child wants to test other materials that come to mind, she can add those to the table:

BULBS LIGHT UP (YES/NO)		
Material Used	Insulator	Conductor
Sewing needle		
Plastic lid		
Styrofoam peanut		
Pencil lead		
Human fingernail		
Human hair		
Stainless steel pot		
Drinking glass		
Ceramic plate		
Wooden toothpick		
Salted water (add 1 teaspoon of salt in any cup, and fill to the top)		

Help her recognize the two categories of materials she used: those that allowed the light bulbs to light up, and those that didn't. Now ask her to think about which of those materials she used in the circuit would count as conductors. In other words, which are the *conductors* and which are the *insulators*? Have her go through the list, checking the appropriate box—insulator or conductor—for each material she tested.

The electric circuit is closed when you connect a conducting object between the two loose wires. In such a closed circuit, the light bulbs light up when *every* part of the circuit is made of a conductor. If there is one insulator along the path, the bulbs won't light up.

STEM Q&A

What makes charges move in an electric circuit?

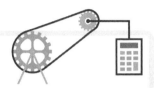

A power source is what makes charges flow in a circuit. A battery is an example of a power source. The battery "kicks" the charges and moves them through it, like a soccer player kicks a ball as he passes it on. The charges maintain this current flow in the circuit as long as the battery is not dead.

Conductors allow electric charges to flow through them like traffic flows on the highway. This flow of charges is known as an electric current. When an *insulator* is present, it's like reaching a road that's not finished: No cars could go down such a road. The electric charges can't move along such a path, and there's no electric current in the circuit.

STEM Words to Know

electrolyte

An electrolyte is a substance that has an electric charge because it has *ions*. For example, when dissolving table salt in water, the sodium and chlorine atoms (which were sharing an electron) dissociate from each other, creating a positively charged sodium ion and a negatively charged chlorine ion. Such a solution is called an electrolyte.

Your daughter might have thought of testing human skin in the circuit, and may have found out that the bulbs didn't light up. Even though the human body is a conductor (because it's made of mostly water that has electrolytes), it's a poor conductor when using a power source like a battery. That's why it's safe to place a finger in this circuit. Do not use a power source like an electric outlet.

The reason a 4.5V battery pack doesn't cause a shock but a 110V electric outlet does lies in the strength of the electric current generated by these power sources. When connecting to the battery pack that's connected to the two light bulbs, the batteries generate a very small current that's harmless. When connecting to the electric outlet, the current generated is much, much greater and could be lethal.

Electrical Engineer

Electrical engineers work on electrical equipment. They design equipment such as communication systems, navigation systems, energy production systems, motors, and radar, as well as equipment that is directly related to power generation and distribution. In addition, they develop the equipment, oversee its manufacturing process, and then test it before it is made available to the consumer.

Different careers are available for electrical engineers. For example, in communications systems they would develop equipment that transmits digital signals to cell phones. They would also design electrical grids that would help conserve energy. In energy production systems, they would develop sustainable energy technology for harvesting power.

ACTIVITY:

ELECTRICITY AND MAGNETISM: THE TWO SISTERS

Some phenomena in nature can't occur without some associated effect happening at the same time. For example, every time the sun comes up over the eastern horizon at sunrise, it's automatic that there'll be light everywhere. The sunrise and the lighting effect are associated because of the very nature of the sun, which is to illuminate.

Electricity and magnetism constitute a similar example. When we have electricity moving in wires, magnetic effects show up immediately. The two are like sisters that can't be separated. How can such a phenomenon be observed, and can it be useful in some everyday life application?

MATERIALS NEEDED:
- 2 miniature light bulbs rated 2.5V 0.3A
- 2 miniature bulb holders with plastic circular bases
- 3 size-D batteries
- Electrical tape
- 3 alligator clip wires
- Liquid-filled compass
- Clear tape

PROCEDURE:
1. Using the electrical tape, assist your child in securing the 3 D batteries in a row end to end. Make sure the positive end (labeled +) of one battery is snuggled tightly against the negative end (labeled –) of the next battery. Now the battery pack is ready.

2. Assist your child in taping one end of an alligator clip wire to one end of the battery pack. Then help her tape another alligator clip wire to the other end of the battery pack.

3. Ask your child to screw each light bulb into the bulb holders so they can be ready for use. Assist her in noticing how each bulb holder has two metal ears (as shown in the following figure) where alligator clip wires can be attached.

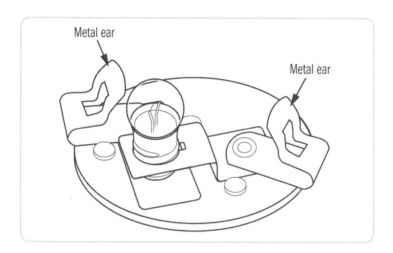

Metal ear

Metal ear

4. Using the wire attached to the positive side of the battery pack, clip the loose end of that wire onto the metal ear of one of the bulb holders.

5. Next, connect the loose wire on the negative side of the battery pack to the metal ear of the other bulb holder.

6. Now tell your child to use the third alligator clip wire and connect it to the other metal ear of the bulb holder on the right. Leave the other side of this wire loose for the time being.

7. Now it's time for your child to use the compass. Ask her to place the compass flat on the table, beside the bulbs. Tell her to place the loose wire on top of the compass. Assist her in

lining up the loose wire exactly parallel to the compass needle, as shown in the following diagram. Once the loose wire and the compass needle are in alignment, use the clear tape to tape the wire onto the compass needle. Also tape both wire and compass onto the table so they don't move.

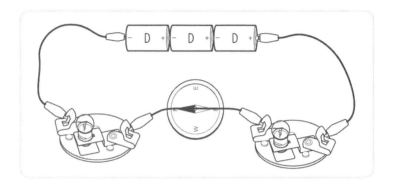

8. Tell your child that she's now ready to connect the loose end of the wire to the left bulb holder's empty ear that's not connected to the battery. Before she does that, tell her to focus on the compass. Once she connects that wire, both light bulbs should light up. What do you both observe happening to the compass needle the instant she connects the wire?

The light bulbs light up, showing that electricity is indeed moving through the wires. But there's another effect associated with the moving electricity. This other effect shows up in the compass needle that moves (or deflects)!

But isn't a compass used to detect a magnetic field? After all, people carry compasses so they can find the direction they need to travel in, especially if they're hiking in the wilderness. The compass responds to the presence of the earth's magnetic field, aligning its needle with the direction north. Some people even like to play with the compass needle by bringing a magnet nearby and watching the needle respond to the magnet. So what does a battery and a bunch of wires and bulbs have to do with magnetism? After all, your child didn't bring a magnet near the compass.

Every time there's electricity moving in the wires, there's automatically a magnetic field that shows up at the same time. Electricity and magnetism can't be separated. The magnetic field shows up right around the wires. That's why the wire had to be laid right on top of the compass. Since the compass responds to the presence of a magnetic field (as it does to Earth's magnetic field), it can actually detect the magnetic field close by in the wires.

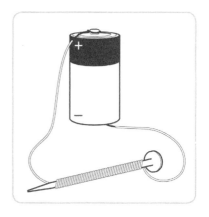

Simple electromagnet

Can this phenomenon be put to good use? Can a magnetic field generated by electricity be fashioned into something useful? One very important and useful tool is an electromagnet (as in electric magnet). All one needs in order to make an electromagnet is to wrap the wire many times around an object made of iron, such as an iron nail, and connect the two ends of the wire to a battery. It's as simple as that!

Electromagnets

Electromagnets are used in many places. For example, if one needs to have a magnet he can turn on or off when needed, he uses an electromagnet. Electromagnets are used in junkyards when heavy objects such as cars need to be lifted and moved around. The electromagnet is turned on when the car is ready to be lifted. When the electromagnet is turned off, the car drops into the location it needs to sit. If a permanent magnet were used, it would be near impossible to "peel" the car off that giant permanent magnet once the magnet was fastened to it.

Mechanical Engineer

Mechanical engineers design devices such as machines and tools. A mechanical engineer has the role of taking an idea and developing it into a product that is ready for the marketplace. Examples of machines that mechanical engineers build include cars, engines, generators, turbines, elevators, escalators, refrigeration and air conditioning systems, and robots used in manufacturing, among many others. In addition, mechanical engineers are involved in the process of developing the machines and tools they design and seeing them through the manufacturing process, as well as testing them afterward.

Mechanical engineering is one of the broadest fields of engineering. The skills mechanical engineers would have acquired upon graduation with a bachelor's degree make them immediately hirable.

ACTIVITY:
BALLOON-POWERED CAR

Vehicles today are powered in so many different ways. There are gasoline-fueled automobiles, and ones that run on diesel. Solar cars do exist, even if they're mostly student projects in university-level engineering classes. Electric cars have been making their way onto the scene, and hydrogen fuel cell cars are also a reality.

Since the invention of the wheel, earlier people have relied on animals to supply the power for movement. But today new transportation technologies are being developed that would've seemed like science fiction only a few decades ago.

Are there simpler ways to power a vehicle—even simpler than using an animal? The answer is yes. You can actually use your own breath; but, of course, the vehicle would have to be a toy car in order for it to move. The idea behind this experiment is that you and your child can build a car from scratch and use an "alternative source of energy" to power it.

MATERIALS NEEDED:
- Balloon
- 1 regular drinking straw
- 2 acrylic straws 9" in length
- Tape
- 3"-wide double-sided tape
- 4 blank CDs
- 8 identical plastic caps or lids (from juice bottles or milk containers)
- Wooden skewers 10" in length
- Rectangular balsa wood sheet (¼" thick) 10" × 4"
- Awl, or other hole-poking tool
- Ruler or tape measure
- Utility knife

- Glue gun
- Glue sticks (for glue gun)

PROCEDURE:

1. If the balsa wood sheet is longer than 10", use the utility knife to cut a 10" length of that 4"-wide sheet. This is the body of the car.
2. Cut the acrylic straws to 6" each.
3. Using the glue gun, demonstrate to your child how to attach the first acrylic straw to the front edge of the balsa wood sheet. Make sure to center the straw along that edge. Assist your child as he attaches the other thick-walled straw to the back edge of the balsa wood sheet.
4. Assist your child in poking holes through the centers of the plastic caps.
5. Using the hot-glue gun, help your child glue a plastic cap (with the open side of the cap facing the CD) onto the center of the CD. Make sure the hole in the center of the cap is lined up with the center of the CD. The plastic cap is like a hubcap. Ask your child to place another plastic cap on the other side of the same CD, so that the CD has a hubcap on each side.
6. Place the remaining 6 plastic caps on the other 3 CDs in the same fashion. The wheels of the car are ready.
7. Using the skewers, push one skewer through the holes of the "hubcaps" of one of the wheels. The holes poked into the plastic lids should be just big enough to allow the skewer to go through snugly.
8. Tell your child to slide the skewer through the straw mounted along the front of the body of his car (the front edge of the balsa wood sheet).
9. Next, ask your child to push the other end of the skewer into the holes of another one of the wheels, so that he has both front wheels mounted. The skewer should fit snugly onto the second hubcap. Push the two wheels close to the straw

ends, but leave just enough wiggle room for the skewer to rotate freely inside the straw.

10. Ask your child to follow the same steps to mount the rear wheels onto the body of his car. Trim off the excess skewer length outside the front and rear "hubcaps," leaving about ½".

11. Next, tell your child to slide the regular straw slightly into the balloon, then tape the balloon securely onto the straw.

12. Using the double-sided tape, ask your child to wrap the tape once all the way around the width of the balsa wood (the body of the car) and fasten the two ends of the tape on the back side.

13. To perform the experiment, find a long, smooth floor surface (such as a wooden or smooth concrete floor). Have your child place the car on the floor at one end of the long surface.

14. It is testing time! Tell your child to blow into the balloon through the straw until it is fully inflated. Tell him to place his thumb at the end of the straw to cover it until he's ready to launch the car. Have him place the balloon with the attached straw onto the sticky tape on the car so that the balloon itself touches the tape and the straw lines up along the length of the car. When he's ready, tell him to let go of the straw and observe what happens to the car.

How far does the car go? Is the room long enough to allow for the balloon to deflate fully?

This type of car is obviously not meant to keep going very long like the ones that use batteries, but hopefully your child will have a good time with this car he created himself.

POWERING A BOAT WITH SOAP

Boats can be powered by a person rowing tirelessly until he gets to his destination. Boats can also be powered by the wind, or by gasoline.

Believe it or not, you can power a boat using something as simple as soap, and it's all related to the surface tension of water. A liquid like water has *surface tension* when it is in contact with the air. The molecules in the water are much more attracted to each other (they stick together) than to the air around them. The water molecules pull so strongly toward each other that they act as if there is an elastic sheet stretched around them. When an object is placed in water, the surface tension of the water surrounding the object is all the same, so the object doesn't move. But if something can make the surface tension in the rear of a boat smaller than in the front of it, the greater surface tension in the water in the front can pull the boat forward.

This idea was demonstrated by scientists using soap. Soap lowers the surface tension of water. That's why soap feels slippery on the skin, and spreads easily. If there is a reservoir in the rear of a light boat that releases soap into the water behind the boat, the spreading soap lowers the surface tension behind the boat, allowing the water in front of the boat (with higher tension) to pull the boat forward.

MATERIALS NEEDED:

- ⅛" polystyrene foam sheet
- Scissors or a craft knife
- Dishwasher soap
- Small glass
- Teaspoon
- Liquid dropper

- Long basin filled with water (about 25"–30" in length)
- Rubbing alcohol

PROCEDURE:

1. Using the drawing to the right as a template, assist your child in cutting a piece of the polystyrene foam in the exact shape and size of the diagram (you might suggest to your child to trace the exact shape onto a piece of paper, then use that paper to draw the shape onto the polystyrene foam). This is the small boat that will be powered by soap. The boat should be about 1.5" in length and 1" in width at the base.

2. Fill the basin with water. Ask your child to place her polystyrene mini boat on the surface of the water.

3. Tell your child to pour about 4 tablespoons of the dishwasher soap into the small glass and add some water, then stir with the spoon. This will create a liquid soap that she can add to the boat with the dropper.

4. Draw some of the liquid soap into the dropper and then squeeze the liquid soap into the hole in the back of the boat. The hole acts like the soap reservoir for the boat. What does the boat do? Does it move forward for a short spurt? Does the boat then stop afterward?

You just witnessed how the difference in surface tension between the water in front and behind the boat propelled it forward. This difference in surface tension was created by the soap. Unfortunately, the soap acts like a surfactant, spreading over the water and lowering the water's surface tension all around the boat. That's why the boat stops. In order to make the boat move forward again, you'd have to replace the water in the basin with new water that has no soap in it.

That's not fun! Is there another way to make the boat move forward constantly? In 2013, a team in the United Kingdom demonstrated that other liquids besides soap can be used to lower the surface tension of water behind the boat. They used rubbing alcohol!

Have your child repeat the experiment again. This time, tell her to use a clean dropper to add a couple of drops of rubbing alcohol into the hole in the rear end of the boat. Does the boat move forward? If so, tell her to add another couple of drops into the boat's reservoir (the hole). Is the boat propelled forward again? Tell her to keep adding more drops of alcohol, and notice that she doesn't need to replace the water in the basin like she did when she used soap.

The reason alcohol works better than soap is because the alcohol lowers the surface tension behind the boat, but—unlike the soap—alcohol doesn't spread over the surface of the water all around the boat; rather, it mixes with the water. This way the water can keep its higher surface tension.

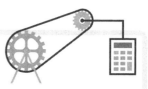

STEM Q&A

What are visible signs of water surface tension?

A water droplet is spherical in shape. This is due to the strong attraction between water molecules. The molecules in a water drop pull inwardly toward each other with an equal amount of force, creating a spherical shape to the water drop, and tension on its surface. So the fact that a water droplet is a sphere *is* a visible sign of water surface tension.

It's true the boat is a miniature, but it serves the purpose of demonstrating yet another scientific principle. Surface tension of a liquid like water is an important phenomenon behind why water droplets are spherical in shape. It's also the reason some bugs are able to "glide" on the surface of water.

MOUSETRAP CAR RACE

Moving objects that are powered usually have some form of stored energy that can be converted into motion (and often heat). For example, when you push a heavy object in order to move it, you're able to do so only because you gave your body food earlier that day. The source of the energy behind the work you did was stored in the food you ate. In other words, energy is constantly transforming from one form into another.

The gasoline you put into your car's tank has stored energy in it. Once that gasoline is ignited inside the engine, the stored energy in the gasoline transforms into work that eventually turns the car's axles. There are other ways energy can be stored to power vehicles. One such way is the energy stored in the wound torsion spring of a mousetrap. It's true that you can only power a small vehicle with a mousetrap spring, but the principle is the same. You're transforming the stored energy in the wound spring into power for the toy car.

MATERIALS NEEDED:
- Old-fashioned spring-loaded mousetrap
- 4 blank CDs
- 8 identical plastic caps or lids (from juice bottles or milk containers)
- 2 jumbo-sized safety pins
- 1 acrylic straw
- Wooden skewers (⅛" diameter)
- Rectangular balsa wood sheet (¼" thick) 14" × 4"
- Plastic clothes hanger
- Fishing line
- Cable ties
- Awl, or other hole-poking tool

- Ruler or tape measure
- Utility knife
- Wire cutter
- Scissors
- Athletic tape
- Glue gun
- Glue sticks (for glue gun)

PROCEDURE:

1. If the balsa wood sheet is longer than 14", then use the utility knife to cut a 14" length of that 4"-wide sheet. This is the body of the car.
2. Using the utility knife, cut out a rectangular notch from the rear end of the balsa wood frame. The notch should be 1" deep and 2" wide, as shown in the following diagram.

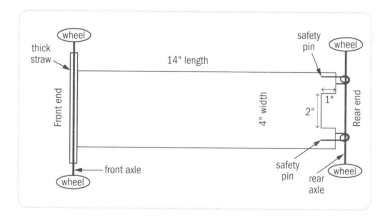

3. Using the glue gun, assist your child in securing the acrylic straw to the front edge of the balsa wood sheet. Make sure to center the straw along that edge.
4. Using the wire cutter, cut off the fastening ends of the jumbo safety pins. This will take some force, so you might want to do that task yourself.

5. Now use the hot-glue gun to securely fasten the long ends of each safety pin on the top and the bottom of the rear end of the car frame. **IMPORTANT: Make sure the holes of the pins line up perfectly face-to-face. The rear axle will slide through those two holes.**

6. Now it's time to make the wheels of the car. Assist your child in poking holes through the centers of the plastic caps.

7. Using the hot-glue gun, glue a plastic cap (with the open side of the cap facing the CD) onto the center of the CD. Make sure the center of the cap is lined up with the center of the CD. The plastic cap is like a hubcap. Ask your child to place another plastic cap on the other side of the same CD, so that the CD has a hubcap on each side.

8. Place the remaining 6 plastic caps on the other 3 CDs in the same fashion. The wheels of the car are ready.

9. Using one of the skewers, push the end of that skewer through the hole in the hubcap of one of the wheels. The hole poked into the plastic caps should be just big enough to allow the skewer to go through **snugly**.

10. Tell your child to slide the free end of the skewer through the straw mounted on the front end of his car.

11. Next, ask your child to push the other end of that skewer into the hole of another one of the wheels, so that he has both front wheels mounted. The skewer should fit **snugly** onto the second hubcap. Push the two wheels toward the straw ends, but leave just enough wiggle room for the skewer to rotate freely inside the straw.

12. Ask your child to slide the second skewer through the mounted safety pins in the rear of the car, and center it. This skewer will serve as the rear axle that will be powered by the mousetrap. NOTE: Do *not* mount the rear wheels yet.

13. Using the athletic tape, cut a foot-length of the tape and wind it around the center of the rear axle until the tape makes a thick padding that's ¼" in thickness.

14. Secure a cable tie strongly over the center of the athletic tape, then cut the excess cable with scissors. The tie will serve as a notch to loop the fishing line around. Use the glue gun to further secure the cable tie over the tape so that the tie does not move, wiggle, slide, or rotate. Make sure to *not* cover the tie notch with any glue, so that the notch sticks out.

15. Next, have your child place the rear wheels onto the rear axle as he did with the front wheels.

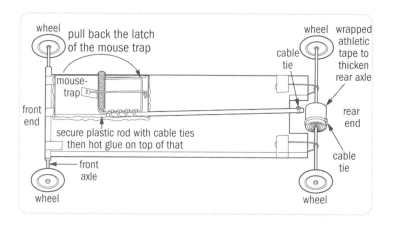

16. Now it's time to make a few adjustments to the mousetrap. Using the utility knife, cut out the bottom horizontal part of the plastic hanger. You need about a 12" length plastic rod. This is something you might want to do yourself, since it will take a lot of effort.

17. It's now critical to figure out where to attach the plastic rod onto the mousetrap. After loading the mousetrap, hold it so that the metal latch is close to you, and the side the latch will snap onto is on the far side. The plastic rod will need to be attached to the left arm of the latch, as shown in the diagram. Assist your child in tying the plastic rod onto the left metal arm of the mousetrap using cable ties. Cut off the

excess cables, and secure the cable ties onto the mousetrap arm using hot glue.

18. Next, fasten a cable tie about an inch from the tip of the plastic rod. Cut off the excess cable and hot glue the cable tie onto the rod securely.

19. Now it's time to secure the mousetrap to the frame of the car. Using the hot-glue gun, place the loaded mousetrap plus plastic rod at the front right corner of the car frame, as shown in the diagram.

20. Carefully release the load from the mousetrap so the plastic rod faces forward, toward the front of the car. This will help your child assess how much fishing line to use. Tell him to tie one end of the fishing line around the plastic rod below the cable tie. Tell him to tie the fishing line a couple of times, then secure it to the rod with hot glue.

21. Ask your child to extend the fishing line all the way to the rear axle where the cable tie is. Tell him to cut his line a little longer than where it reaches the axle so that he has enough excess line to make a loop. Make a loop at the end of the fishing line.

22. Now it's time for your child to power his car with the mousetrap. With the plastic rod facing the front of the car, tell your child to put the fishing line loop around the cable-tie notch in the rear axle. Assist him in turning the rear wheels so that the fishing line starts winding around the wrapped athletic tape on the rear axle. This should start lifting the plastic rod that's extended from the mousetrap arm. Tell him to keep winding the fishing line around the rear axle until the plastic rod moves all the way back and it is lying down along the frame of the car. Tell him to hold the rear wheels so that he prevents them from rotating. His car is now ready to be tested.

23. Tell your child to stand at one end of a long hallway with a smooth surface and place the car on the floor.

24. It is testing time! Tell your child to let go of the rear wheels.

How far does his car travel before it stops? Measure the distance and record it.

Ask your child to make another mousetrap car, but use a shorter plastic rod (perhaps 8" long). Have him race both cars side by side. Do they both travel just as far? Which one travels the farthest? He probably found out that the car with the longer rod travels farther.

These investigations can become the entry point into the world of design that has intrigued engineers for centuries. The mousetrap car can be the first of many design projects that engage your child for a long time to come.

Automotive Engineer

Automotive engineering is one branch of mechanical engineering. Automotive engineers are involved in the design and development of cars, trucks, motorcycles, and any other vehicles that use motors. They also see such vehicles through the manufacturing and testing process.

This is a very specialized field, and few universities offer bachelor degrees in automotive engineering. In general, students start by majoring in mechanical engineering, and choose an emphasis in automotive engineering by taking classes in this area. Such courses might include internal combustion engines, diesel engine theory, and powertrain dynamics. There are many more universities that offer master's degrees in automotive engineering for those interested in earning a graduate degree in the field.

ACTIVITY:
WATER ROCKET LAUNCH

Rockets are a fascination for many. Is there an easy way to make a rocket that's safe to launch in your own neighborhood park? Absolutely. The best such rocket is a water-air rocket. When air is compressed inside a partially filled water bottle, the built-up pressure inside the bottle becomes too large at some point, and the bottle launches into the air like a rocket. Try this experiment outside on a warm day where there's plenty of open space around you.

MATERIALS NEEDED:
- Empty 1-liter soda bottle
- Bicycle pump with hose (one that can stand upright)
- Electrical tape
- 6"-long PVC pipe (3" in diameter)
- Hacksaw

PROCEDURE:
1. Assist your child in covering the outside edge of the loose end of the bicycle pump hose with electrical tape so that it can fit tightly into the mouth of the soda bottle.
2. Using the hacksaw, help your child cut out a small square window at one end of the PVC pipe right at the edge, so only three cuts need to be made. The PVC pipe will serve as a vertical launcher for the bottle rocket. The window will allow your child to insert the hose of the bicycle pump into the PVC pipe.
3. Tell your child to fill ⅓ of the bottle with water.
4. Ask your child to thread the bicycle pump hose into the PVC pipe through the little cut-out window and out the other end. Tell her to stand the PVC pipe on the ground so that the window is resting on the ground. The PVC pipe should be standing upright on its end.

5. Assist your child in tightly fitting the bicycle hose into the mouth of the bottle without spilling any of its water content. Make sure the hose fits really tightly, so you can pump enough air into the bottle to build up plenty of pressure for the launch.

6. Now place the bottle (hose attached) onto the PVC pipe such that the bottle is standing vertically with the mouth of the bottle inserted into the PVC pipe. Make sure the bicycle pump stands on the ground about a foot from where the PVC pipe is standing.

7. Tell your child to start pumping air into the rocket. She'll start to see bubbles form in the water inside the rocket. Make sure she's standing off to the side of the bottle and *not* looking directly down at it. You might want to assist her in pumping air into the bottle. How many pumps does it take before the rocket launches? Can she estimate how high it flew?

8. Your child will want to repeat the launch of her rocket. See if you can wind a few more turns of electrical tape around the end of the pump hose so that you can fit the hose even more tightly into the bottle. The tighter the connection between hose and bottle, the higher the air pressure builds inside the bottle, and the higher the rocket goes.

Aerospace Engineer

Aerospace engineers research, design, develop, and test aircraft (such as planes and jets), spacecraft (such as space vehicles and satellites), and missiles. Their main focus is on the aerodynamics of vehicles that fly within Earth's atmosphere and beyond its boundaries. They can specialize in areas such as structural design, navigation, propulsion, and guidance and control systems. Aerospace engineers can work in private commercial companies or in the military.

MINI PYRAMIDS—MANY TRIANGLES

Lots of young learners are given the opportunity to build miniature pyramids as part of a social studies class project. If your child's teacher doesn't assign the Giza project, you might consider doing it as a family learning activity. Building pyramids is fun, and it provides you with the opportunity to review triangles with your child.

MATERIALS NEEDED:

- Several sheets of card stock
- Ruler
- Scissors
- Glue
- Scotch tape
- Crayons or markers
- Sand (optional)

It's not difficult to build them. There are many approaches you and your child can use. First, you'll have to make basic decisions: How big do you want your pyramids to be? How many pyramids will you build? (The Giza Necropolis has three major pyramids.) How will you decorate them? Once you've made your choices, the rest is fairly straightforward. The purpose of this activity is to use it as an opportunity to review the geometry of triangles with your child.

Triangle Basics

The three interior angles of a triangle always add up to 180 degrees. An *equilateral triangle* has three equal sides and three equal angles (each interior angle is 60 degrees). An *isosceles triangle* has two equal sides and two equal interior angles. A *scalene triangle* has no equal sides and no equal angles.

A triangle can also be categorized based on the measurements of its interior angles. For an *acute triangle*, all of its interior angles are less than 90 degrees. A *right triangle* has one interior angle that's exactly 90 degrees. A *right triangle* also has one side that's longer than the other two sides. It's the side of the triangle opposite from the right angle. That side, the longest side of the right triangle, is known as the *hypotenuse*. An *obtuse triangle* has an interior angle that's greater than 90 degrees.

Back to the Build

To build a miniature pyramid, you'll need four equilateral triangles and a square base. It's best if you measure and draw the pieces on card stock before cutting them out. Help your child measure out and draw four equilateral triangles and a square base. (Note that the square base should be the same width as the bottom edge of the triangles.)

STEM Q&A

Who was Pythagoras?

Pythagoras was a famous mathematician and philosopher who lived in Greece around 500 B.C. Although he and his followers contributed several important ideas to the study of mathematics, Pythagoras is most famous for the Pythagorean theorem, a formula that applies to all right triangles.

After you've drawn the pieces on card stock, cut them out and assemble them using glue. You may need to use Scotch tape on the inside so that the pieces hold together while the glue is drying.

Another approach to decorating the pyramid is to cover the sides in glue after the pieces are assembled, and coat the pyramid with real sand. This approach can get messy, so you'll want to do it outside or over a large piece of cardboard or plastic. The sand approach, though messy, results in a more realistic-looking miniature pyramid.

More Pyramid Activities

Ask your child if he thinks he could build a pyramid using an isosceles or scalene triangle. Encourage him to test his prediction building a mini pyramid with these other triangle shapes. Either while building or after the initial build, you can help your child find the area of one of the triangles used in the pyramid construction. The area of a triangle is found by multiplying the base by the height and dividing the product in half. For example, if your triangle has a base of 4" and a height of 4", the triangle's area is 8 sq." (4 × 4 = 16, half of which is 8).

STEM Words to Know

Pythagorean theorem

The Pythagorean theorem states that, for a right triangle, the square of the hypotenuse is equal to the sum of the squares of the other two sides. The theorem can be written in equation form as $a^2 + b^2 = c^2$, where c is the length of the hypotenuse, and a and b are the lengths of the triangle's other two sides.

The mini pyramid project also provides you with an opportunity to discuss ancient Egyptian history with your child. He may find it interesting to know that, although experts have proposed many theories, no one has quite figured out how the ancient Egyptians constructed the actual pyramids. One thing is certain, however: Those ancient builders had a supreme understanding of geometry.

Industrial Engineer

Industrial engineering is concerned with optimizing systems that include equipment, people, materials, energy, and information, as well as money. The work of industrial engineers involves identifying where wastefulness occurs in a system, then finding solutions to reduce it. Industrial engineers often work in manufacturing and technical services.

CHAPTER 3

PHYSICS AND ASTRONOMY

Physics is everywhere around us. You've always had a direct experience of it even if you were not aware of it. You experienced physics every time you sat in a bathtub full of water. You definitely felt it every time you moved a box or heavy object, or when you went bowling with family or friends.

Astronomy is the oldest of the sciences known to us. Celestial objects have always intrigued human beings. Since the dawn of our species' existence, humans have relied on those heavenly objects to navigate through space and to identify the seasons.

This chapter will help you and your child explore some examples of the physics principles that surround you, many of which show up in your own home. In addition, this chapter introduces some basic concepts in astronomy and highlights some of the careers available to people who study physics or astronomy.

RACING JUICE CANS

Sir Isaac Newton was an English physicist and mathematician who is considered by many physicists to be the father of classical physics. He was born in England in 1643 and died in 1727. He was once sitting under an apple tree when an apple fell on his head and led him to formulate the universal law of gravitation. According to Newton's first law, sometimes called the law of inertia, when an object is in motion it wants to stay in that same motion, unless a force acts on it to make it change. This also means that if an object is *not* moving, it wants to remain still unless a force acts on it. For example, if you place an ice cube on a horizontal surface—perhaps in a baking pan on your kitchen countertop—it will stay put. But if you tilt the pan and let the force of gravity act on the cube, it will most definitely move.

Physicist

Physicists study the science of physics, which attempts to understand the laws that govern nature. Physicists explore all aspects of matter and energy, as well as the interaction between them. Some of the topics studied in physics are space and time, electricity, magnetism, relativity, and thermodynamics.

Physicists specialize in some specific field, such as particle physics, nuclear physics, biological physics, optical physics, condensed-matter physics, and astrophysics. Theoretical physicists, such as Albert Einstein, explore the theory underlying principles in nature. They rely heavily on mathematics to construct models that explain natural phenomena. Experimental physicists, like Marie Curie, work in laboratories conducting experiments in order to observe physical phenomena.

It's a property of matter to want to keep moving if already in motion, or to remain still if it's not moving. In other words, when it comes down to motion or stillness, matter always, always, always *resists* change.

The motion of the ice cube moving across the baking pan is called *sliding*, or *translational*, motion. But what if an object rolls instead of slides? Does Newton's first law still apply? A simple experiment will yield the answer.

MATERIALS NEEDED:
- 2 identical cans of frozen fruit juice concentrate
- 1 wooden board, 1½' × 4'
- Stack of books or magazines

The question this experiment will investigate is whether matter—in this case, the juice inside the can—resists change in its motion more when it's in liquid form or when it's in solid form. The real question is whether it's easier for the juice to go downhill when it's *sliding* inside the can because it's a liquid, or when it's *rolling* with the can because the juice is frozen.

To prepare for the experiment, keep one of the frozen fruit juice concentrate cans in the freezer and allow the other to sit on your countertop for a day so that it completely thaws.

When the cans are ready, prop the wooden board up on one end using a stack of books or magazines. This will create the incline necessary for racing the two cans.

Before proceeding with the experiment, ask your child to make a prediction about the results. Which do you think will reach the bottom of the incline first, the frozen juice or the liquid juice? Remember that the frozen juice will *roll* down the incline, while the liquid juice will *slide* inside the can. Talk with your child about how this could impact the movement of the cans.

After you've made your prediction, place the two cans side by side at the top of the incline. Use a ruler to line up the two cans so that when you remove the ruler, the cans will begin their downhill descent at the same time.

Ready . . . set . . . let go!

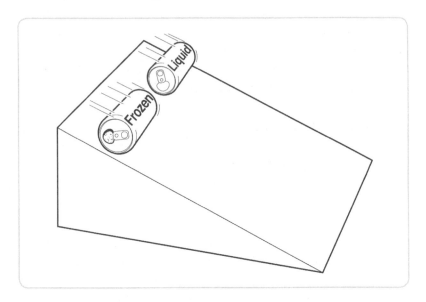

The result might surprise you both. You might have predicted that the frozen can would reach the bottom first, but it turns out to be the opposite!

Since the liquid juice can reaches the bottom faster, the conclusion can be made that it's easier for the juice to *slide* inside the can than it is to *roll* inside the can. Since it's easier for the can containing the liquid juice to get to the bottom, the conclusion can also be made that the liquid-juice can resists change in its motion *less* than the frozen-juice can.

The result of this experiment reveals that it's easier to slide than to roll, which is something you can definitely feel when a car's tires lock up and start sliding on an icy road.

Repeat the racing juice cans experiment for a friend or family member. See if your friend or family member can predict which juice will win the race.

ACTIVITY:

EXPLORING NEWTON'S THIRD LAW

You might have heard the statement "For every action there is an equal and opposite reaction." This *law of force pairs* is what we call Newton's third law. This is because when a first object acts on a second object with a force, the second object automatically does the same back, but in the opposite direction. Specifically, the force from Object 1 cannot show up on its own without the opposite force from Object 2 showing up as well. They are always *paired*. If you wonder where in your daily life you can observe this principle, here are a few hints: Newton's third law is what makes a space shuttle fly up and away from the earth, and it's also what makes you able to stand up from a seated position. How does this principle work?

MATERIALS NEEDED:
- 1 balloon
- Masking tape
- 1 drinking straw
- 1 bag clip sealer

PROCEDURE:
1. Tell your child to insert the straw about 1½" into the neck of the balloon.
2. Assist your child in securing the straw at the opening of the balloon, so that the opening is totally taped onto the straw with no gaps.
3. Have your child blow through the straw to inflate the balloon so that it's full to the max.
4. Once the balloon is fully inflated, help your child clip the straw with the clip sealer so that the air is sealed tight inside the balloon.
5. Ask your child to stand at one end of a long table or wooden floor (a hallway is ideal), and place the balloon so that the straw is lined up parallel to the length of the hall or table.

6. Now tell your child to block the end of the straw with her finger to prevent the air from escaping, and release the clip sealer. Ready, set . . . let go. What do you observe?

Did the balloon move along the floor like it had a small turbo engine attached to it? Well, in a way it does! But what exactly happened? Here is where Newton's third law comes to the rescue.

When the air inside the balloon begins to release and move out through the straw, the air is actually being forced out by the balloon's deflation. In other words, the balloon pushes the air out. This is the *action* force. The *reaction* force is the force that the air pushes back on the balloon, so the balloon begins to move. Those two action and reaction forces are what Newton's third law is all about. Without the reaction force showing up, the balloon would never have moved!

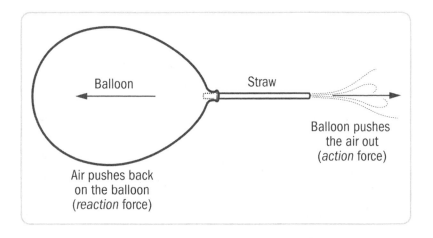

Balloon

Straw

Balloon pushes
the air out
(*action* force)

Air pushes back
on the balloon
(*reaction* force)

This is exactly how the space shuttle is able to move up into the sky. The engine attached to the shuttle pushes the exhaust gases out *downwardly* (*action*). In response, the gases push back *upwardly* on the shuttle and its attached engine (*reaction*). The *action* force acts *on the gases* as they are being expelled downward, and the *reaction* force acts *on the shuttle* being propelled upward.

Newton's cradle

Newton's cradle is a set of steel balls (often five or seven balls) that are hanging right next to each other at the same height. When you lift an end ball off to the side then release it, it strikes the ball adjacent to it, transferring the action and reaction forces to the ball on the far end. That ball, in turn, moves off to the side.

Here's another example from your everyday life where you'll find Newton's third law at work. Next time you find yourself attempting to stand up from being seated in a chair, become aware of Newton's third law *action* and *reaction* force pairs. As you attempt to stand, you actually push downward on the floor with your feet. This is the *action*. The *reaction* is the floor pushing back on your feet, helping you to stand up. Think about this: If your feet were pushing downward on a floor that can't push back up, like a thick layer of mud, would you be able to stand up? If the floor's *reaction* that pushes back on your feet were to vanish, you would be stuck in your chair!

Nuclear Physicist

Nuclear physicists focus their investigations on the nucleus of the atom. They explore the subatomic particles that compose the nucleus as well as the forces that hold the nucleus together.

Nuclear physicists can work in careers involving the harnessing of nuclear energy as a form of alternative energy. Such physicists work in nuclear power plants. Another possible career path includes working in radioactive medicine to explore medical applications of nuclear radiation. Nuclear physicists can also be found working in astronomy as well as in archaeology since both fields use radiocarbon dating.

ACTIVITY:
THE VELOCITY OF BOWLING BALLS

Bowling balls are the heaviest balls used in any sport. If you're a small person, you might wonder why there aren't small bowling balls to match your tiny physique. But the truth is that you can't play the game with a small, light ball.

To begin to understand the physics involved in a game of bowling, you must first know something about forces. There are two forces that act on a bowling ball when it's placed on a level wooden floor (such as a bowling lane). There's the force of gravity pulling the ball down, but there's also the force of the floor pushing the ball up to support it.

If the floor weren't hard—if it were made of Jell-O, say—it wouldn't be able to push the ball up hard enough. The force of gravity and the force of the wooden floor are equal in strength, but opposite in direction (one is up and the other is down), so they balance each other and the ball just sits there. If the floor were pushing up harder than the force of gravity pulling down, the ball would float up. Or if the force of gravity were stronger than the force of the floor, the ball would sink into the floor.

What forces affect the bowling ball after you throw it down the bowling lane? Believe it or not, they're exactly the same forces that affect the ball when it's just sitting on the floor or lane. Once the ball leaves your hand and is rolling down the lane, there's the force of gravity pulling it down and the force of the floor pushing it up, and they're exactly equal but opposite in direction. Note that there's very little friction from the floor because the bowling lane is so smooth. The friction is so small, like a penny to a hundred-dollar bill, that it's negligible.

You may be thinking that when you roll the bowling ball, your hand gives the ball a force. But there's no way you can "send" a force with the ball. Once it leaves your hand, you have no power over the ball, and definitely no force on it. When you set the bowling ball into motion, what you give it is *velocity*.

So what is it about the bowling ball that keeps it moving once it starts rolling? You don't necessarily have to visit a bowling alley to find out.

MATERIALS NEEDED:
- Bowling ball
- 50 sheets of newspaper (or any other paper)
- Flat, smooth wooden surface 3 yards in length (such as hardwood floor or a wooden table)

Note that if you don't have a bowling ball available, you can try the experiment with a billiard ball.

PROCEDURE:
1. Have your child place the bowling ball on the flat, smooth wooden surface, and give it a tap to make it start rolling. (If you are using a table, make sure you catch the bowling ball before it falls off the edge of the table.)
2. Ask her to crumple the newspapers into a big ball the size of the bowling ball. (If you're using a billiard ball, crumple the newspaper into the size of the billiard ball.)
3. Place the paper ball on the wooden surface, and give it the same tap as you gave the bowling ball.

Did you observe how the bowling ball wanted to keep rolling beyond the 3-yard length of the wooden surface? Did you notice that the paper ball didn't, that it stopped shortly after you tapped it? But they are the same in size. Why didn't they act the same?

Newton's first law (the law of inertia) states that when an object is in motion it stays in motion when all the forces acting on it are balanced. But why does the object stay in motion? The more "stuff" packed into an object, the more it wants to stay in motion.

The "stuff" in any object is called *mass*. The bowling ball has more "stuff" in it than the paper ball, so the bowling ball has a bigger mass than the paper ball. That's also why a bowling ball is heavier than the paper ball, because it has more mass in it.

Once an object with a mass is moving, and as long as the forces on it are balanced, it doesn't want to slow down. It wants to keep moving. That's simply how mass behaves. This property of mass is known as *inertia*.

Condensed-Matter Physicist

Condensed-matter physics is a subfield of physics. It studies the physical properties of different condensed phases of matter (such as solids and liquids).

Condensed-matter physicists are researchers. They use physics laws that include quantum mechanics and electromagnetism to better understand properties of the condensed phases of matter. Some of the experiments in condensed-matter physics include examining the behavior of electrons in material. Researchers in some universities are creating exotic electrons that behave in ways that may lead to new semiconducting, superconducting, and quantum material.

STATIC ELECTRICITY

You've probably reached for a doorknob in the winter after rubbing your feet on carpet, only to get zapped. You may have also been shocked attempting to close your car door after you've slipped out of your car seat. You've perhaps noticed warning signs at gas stations regarding static electricity. What is this thing called static electricity, and why can it be dangerous enough at gas stations that it demands a warning sign? Static electricity is an accumulation of excess electrical charges on an insulated object. The word *static* means "stationary" or "not moving."

Particle Physicist

Particle physics is also known as high-energy physics. It pertains to the study of elementary particles that lie inside the nucleus of the atom. Examples of such particles are quarks, leptons, muons, bosons, neutrinos, and others. Particle physicists work either in theoretical or experimental research.

Theoretical particle physicists require knowledge in theories such as quantum field theory. One area of research for a particle physicist is finding a unified field theory that can explain all physical phenomena. Experimental particle physicists may work in particle accelerator laboratories such as CERN in Switzerland, which is the largest particle accelerator in the world.

In order to understand static electricity, it is helpful to learn about atoms and what they consist of. The classical model of an atom includes two types of particles with electrical charge: *protons* and *electrons*. The protons reside in the center of the atom inside the nucleus. Protons have positive electrical charge. The electrons are negatively charged, and move around the nucleus in orbits like the planets move around the sun. Opposite charges attract, so the electrons (–) are attracted to the protons (+), and the atom stays intact. There is one other type of particle inside the nucleus that is electrically neutral. Such neutral particles are called *neutrons*.

A carbon atom, for example, has 6 positively charged protons (p+) and 6 negatively charged electrons (e–), making it electrically neutral. The carbon atom also has 6 neutrons (n) that do not affect its electrical charge.

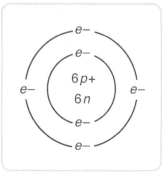

A carbon atom

All objects are made of matter, and matter is made of atoms. When there's an equal number of protons and electrons, there's no excess electrical charge in the object. However, when the object acquires extra charges for some reason, there's an imbalance between the positive and negative charges. This imbalance causes the object to be "charged."

STEM Words to Know

atoms

Atoms are the smallest building block in nature. Everything is made up of atoms. Examples of atoms are helium, calcium, iron, gold, silver, etc. When atoms bond together they form molecules. Examples of molecules are oxygen, hydrogen, carbon dioxide, water, etc.

How can an object become "charged"? Only insulated objects can be charged. For example, plastic, Styrofoam, acrylic, and rubber are all insulated objects that can easily be charged. So if you're wearing shoes with rubber soles, any extra charge your body acquires will stay on you. One way you can get extra charges on your body in the winter (when the air is so dry) is by rubbing your feet against carpet while wearing rubber-soled shoes.

How about an object made of metal; can it be insulated? A metal can be insulated if it's not touching the ground or any non-insulated body. If a metal can be insulated, then it can also be charged. An interesting thing about charged metals is that they make the extra charges sit on the most outside surface of themselves, so they can be as far apart as possible from each other. This is because charges of the same kind repel each other. For example, if one stands on the inside of a charged metal cage and touches the inside of the metal, the extra charges on the outside wall will be out of reach. This means the person won't be zapped when touching the inside wall of an insulated metal cage.

STEM Words to Know

Faraday cage

A Faraday cage is an insulated metal object, like the metal body of a car. At the moment lightning strikes, if a person is only touching the inside of the cage (car), the charges that are discharged by lightning will not transfer to the person and will not cause harm to the person within the cage (car).

Charges that are not paired with opposite ones always strive to find a partner of the opposite kind. When your body has extra electrons in the dry winter from rubbing your feet on the carpet, these electrons need a way to go find other protons to pair with. Since most people don't walk around totally barefoot in the winter with their skin touching the floor, their bodies are insulated by what they wear on their feet. The only opportunity the extra electrons have to escape being trapped on your body is when you touch a metal doorknob. At that instant, all the excess electrons escape your body in a mass exit, and that's when you feel "zapped"!

Similarly, your body can also acquire extra electrons in the dry winter when you brush against your car seat as you slide out of your car. When you have excess electrons on your body, you'll feel the spark the instant you touch the car door. But you can experience static electricity in a manner that's less shocking.

MATERIALS NEEDED:

- Fine-tooth comb
- 1 sheet of paper
- Person who has hair that's more than 5" in length
- Access to a water faucet

PROCEDURE:

1. Do this experiment in the dry winter season. Tell your child to rip the sheet of paper into tiny pieces about ¼" in length and width each, making a small pile of them on the table.

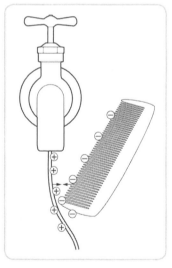

2. Using the comb, ask your child to comb the hair of the designated person who has hair longer than 5".

3. Now bring the comb close to the paper pieces, hovering over them without touching them with the comb. What do you observe? Does the comb pick up some of the torn pieces of paper?

4. Have your child try something else. Ask her to open the water faucet just enough to have a slender continuous stream of water.

5. Tell your child to comb that same hair again, then bring the comb close to the water stream at the top without touching the water. What does she observe?

If your child was amazed by the water stream bending due to the comb's presence, explain that it's the effect of the static electricity that causes this trick. The extra electrons that the comb picked up from the hair attracted some of the protons in the water molecules, bending their path.

Static Electricity Cautions

There was obviously no danger in the simple static electricity experiments described here. So why is there a warning against static electricity spark at gas stations?

Your body gets charged with a lot of extra electrons in the dry winter when rubbing your clothes on the car seat while exiting the car. By the time you stand up outside your car, you're very highly charged. When these charges escape your body at the instant of discharging, they do so very quickly, creating a spark. If there's flammable material connected in some form to your body, for example via the metal handle of the gas nozzle, it could spell disaster.

Here's how you can safely handle yourself. Touch your car door every time you exit your car seat before touching anything else at the gas station. This contact with metal should remove any excess electrical charge that has built up on you.

MAGNETIZING (AND DEMAGNETIZING) A SEWING NEEDLE

Magnets are found everywhere in daily life. You probably have some of them on your refrigerator door glued to the back of a picture or an advertisement. To *magnetize* a metal object means to give it a magnetic property, so that it can pick up some metal objects via attraction. If you use tools a lot, you might prefer magnetized screwdrivers that make it easy to hold screws while placing them where you want them.

Perhaps you've played with magnets at some point in your life to see what kinds of metal objects a magnet can pick up. But what's more fun than playing with a magnet is making one. If you think this is a sophisticated task that requires some serious equipment, you might be surprised.

MATERIALS NEEDED:
- 1 sewing needle
- 4 flat metal-head straight sewing pins
- Strong bar magnet
- Compass

PROCEDURE:
1. If the bar magnet sides are not labeled N (for North) and S (for South), then have your child use the compass needle to identify N and S. Have him bring one side of the bar magnet near the side of the compass needle that's labeled N (it is usually the side that's colored in red). If the N side of the compass needle is attracted to the side of the magnet he brought near it, then that side of the magnet is S (South). Tell your child to make a note of which side of the magnet is S.

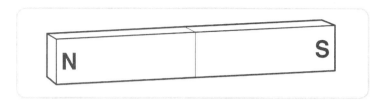

2. Ask your child to scatter the straight pins on a table, just a few inches apart so they are not touching.

3. Tell your child to hold the head of the needle in one hand.

4. Now have him hold the bar magnet in the other hand.

Head of needle

5. Ask your child to stroke the needle, from head to tip, with one side of the bar magnet (say with the north side). Have him do this repeatedly in the same direction at a steady, medium speed, about 5–10 times.

6. Now tell your child to touch the tip of the needle in his hand to one of the straight pins on the table. Ask him to lift up his hand

Tip of needle

holding the needle. Does the needle pick up the pin?

7. Tell your child to see if his needle can pick up more than one of the pins on the table. Ask him to test whether his needle can pick up all four pins at the same time.

By now your child has figured out that he has just made a tiny magnet out of his needle. How exciting! By stroking a metal object like a needle (which is made of steel) with one side of the bar magnet, a permanent magnet is created out of a sewing needle. However, such a magnet is small and weak, so it can only pick up tiny objects like pins and needles. Maybe it would be better to let the needle just be a needle, rather than a magnet. There is a quick way to demagnetize objects. To *demagnetize* a metal object means to make it lose its magnetic property.

MATERIALS NEEDED:
- 1 magnetized sewing needle
- Wand lighter (like a BBQ lighter)
- Pliers

PROCEDURE:
1. Assist your child in holding the head of the needle with a pair of pliers.
2. Lighting the wand lighter, hold the hand of your child that is gripping the pliers in your hand, and bring the needle inside the flame. Keeping the needle in the flame will make it glow. Let the needle glow for about 10 seconds, then set it aside on a piece of paper for a few seconds to cool.
3. Now ask your child to touch the tip of the needle to one of the straight pins on the table. Does the needle pick up the pin?

If most of the needle glowed hot inside the lighter flame, then the needle would have become demagnetized and would no longer pick up the pins. Its magnetic effect was removed by heating it. When the metal of a permanent magnet is heated above what is known as the Curie temperature, it loses its magnetization.

STEM Words to Know

Curie temperature

The Curie temperature, or Curie point, was discovered by a French physicist named Pierre Curie in the late nineteenth century. He worked with his Polish-born wife, Marie Curie, who was also a physicist, working on experiments related to radioactivity.

WHAT ARE MAGNETS MADE OF?

Magnets come in different sizes, shapes, and colors. Some are plated with a silver color, some black, and some even gold, among other colors. But what do they all have in common? Are there certain materials magnets must have inside them to become permanent magnets?

As a rule of thumb, if a magnet cannot strongly attract a particular substance to the point where it will stick to the magnet, then it can never be made out of that substance. For example, if a magnet cannot attract plastic, then a magnet cannot be made out of plastic alone. There are magnets coated with plastic, but the plastic has nothing to do with the magnet being a magnet. So what material is needed to make a permanent magnet?

MATERIALS NEEDED:
- Cylindrical neodymium magnet (½" diameter, 2" length)
- Iron nail
- Penny
- Piece of copper pipe of any size that's available
- Sewing needle
- Pure gold ring
- Pure silver ring
- Small aluminum pan
- Screwdriver
- 2 sheets of paper
- Pencil

Ask your child to make a prediction as to which items may be attracted by the magnet. It's always fun to compare the results of an experiment to a prior prediction.

PROCEDURE:

1. Ask your child to use the two sheets of paper to record her results. Tell her to write at the top of one page the word ATTRACTED, and at the top of the other page the words NOT ATTRACTED.
2. Tell your child to place the objects in the materials list on a table so they are available for her to test them. Ask her to hold the magnet in one hand.
3. Now touch the magnet to each object, one at a time. Ask your child to write the name of each object that sticks to the magnet on the sheet with the ATTRACTED label. Have her remove that object from the magnet so she can be ready to test the next object. All objects not attracted by the magnet should be listed on the other sheet.
4. Have your child test the objects that are not attracted by the magnet twice, so that she can be certain they weren't. If she wants to add other objects to the list, encourage her to do so, and ask her to record them on one of the two data sheets.

Were you surprised by some of the results of this experiment? Did you expect the penny or the copper pipe to stick to the magnet? What about the gold and silver rings and the aluminum pan?

These items just named are metals, and it's easy to assume that all metals would be attracted to a magnet. The penny is copper-plated, but is really made out of zinc, which is another metal. By now your child has figured out that some metals aren't attracted to a magnet. Some of the metals she tested that ended up on her NOT ATTRACTED list were zinc, copper, gold, silver, and aluminum. These are metals that cannot alone be made into a permanent magnet.

Now have her examine the ATTRACTED list. She should find there the iron nail, the sewing needle, and the screwdriver. What material do they all have in common? Ask your child what she thinks.

If your child guessed iron, as the "iron nail" suggests, then she guessed right. Iron is *ferromagnetic*. Ferromagnetic refers to elements that either can become permanently magnetized or are strongly attracted by a permanent magnet. There are three metals that are ferromagnetic: iron, nickel, and cobalt. Other ferromagnetic materials include some rare-earth elements, such as neodymium. The sewing needle and the screwdriver are made of steel, which has iron in it. The sewing needle is also plated with another metal called nickel, which happens to be ferromagnetic as well.

A magnet has a magnetic field. The magnetic field is invisible, but can be felt when bringing the two north sides of two different magnets close to each other. The repulsive effect between the two close north poles that refuse to touch indicates the presence of a magnetic field that is "sensed" by them at a distance.

When a magnet is brought close to an item that contains ferromagnetic material, the ferromagnetic material "senses" the presence of the magnetic field. The ferromagnetic material reacts to the presence of the magnetic field by becoming strongly attracted by it. In other words, once the magnet is at a certain distance from the item, the item starts to move toward the magnet as it is guided by the magnetic field of that magnet.

STEM Words to Know

permanent magnet

A permanent magnet is made out of ferromagnetic material. Once it becomes magnetized, a ferromagnetic material does not lose its magnetic property easily unless heated above a certain high temperature.

Since the items that contained ferromagnetic material were strongly attracted to the magnet, then the material those items are made of can be used to make a permanent magnet. Most magnets nowadays are not made of one element alone. Magnets today are made of an alloy (which is a combination of different elements) that must contain ferromagnetic material.

KEEPING A MOON-PHASE JOURNAL

When the moon is visible at night, it's the brightest object in the night sky. People in ancient cultures were constantly aware of the cycle of the moon as it changed its phase, and this information was significant to their daily lives. Some calendars today still follow the moon's cycle, such as the Jewish and Islamic calendars. There are still indigenous peoples around the globe who use the moon as a method to count elapsed time in lunar cycles. The moon's cycle was important not only for religious purposes, but also for telling time and for navigational purposes.

These days there are so many distractions in everyday life that people rarely look up at the sky, let alone take note of the presence of the moon. It's very simple to learn to become aware of the moon's phases, and to learn to tell time, and directions, simply from the moon. It all starts with keeping a moon journal for one full cycle of the moon.

MATERIALS NEEDED:
- 4 sheets of paper
- Pencil
- Internet access (for cloudy days)

PROCEDURE:
1. Using a search engine on the Internet, find out when the next new moon will be. (A moon cycle is generally considered to begin with the new moon.) Have your child start his observations of the moon on that day.
2. Help your child create a table with four columns on his paper sheets. Ask him to make 30 rows in the table, one for every day of observation. (He will most likely need to use more than one sheet of paper for the entire table.) The provided

table can serve as an example to illustrate what his table would look like. He will need to expand this table into 30 rows to accommodate every day of the lunar cycle.

3. Tell your child he does not need to stay up late or wake up very early on the days when the moon rises and/or sets at times outside his normal waking hours. Assist him in finding the rising and setting times with an Internet search for those days. He can simply search for "data for moon on" and type the date, including the year as well as the city where you live.

4. On days or evenings that are clear, walk outside with your child and observe the moon's shape if it is visible that day or night.

5. Have your child record the moon's data for each day in his table. Assist him in making it a daily habit to either step outside to look for the moon or (in case of cloudy days or days when the moon is not visible during his waking hours) find moon information for that day online.

Use this sample table to help your child make an expanded version for all the days in the moon's cycle. In the column that lists the shape of the moon, have your child draw the shape of the moon for that day.

SAMPLE MOON-PHASES RECORD			
Day Number	Shape of Moon	Moonrise Time	Moonset Time
1			
2			
3			

Once an entire lunar cycle is recorded (from one new moon to the next new moon), look at his record.

Ask your child first to examine the Shape of Moon column in his table. Quiz him on whether he notices more of the moon's disk becoming illuminated with each subsequent day until the full moon. Prompt him to notice what happens to the moon's illumination in the second half of the cycle following the full moon phase. Does he observe that the disk of the moon becomes less and less illuminated as the moon goes through the second half of its cycle?

Next, have your child examine the Moonrise Time column. What does he notice about the rising time of the moon day after day? Ask him if he observes that the moon rises later every day. Ask him to calculate the number of minutes the moon rises later every day. Using a separate sheet of paper, tell your child to start at the top of his table, subtract the moonrise time in the first row from that in the second row, and write the difference on a new sheet of paper. Ask him next to subtract the moonrise time in the second row from that in the third row and record it underneath the first difference he calculated. Tell him to do the same calculation for all subsequent numbers in the Moonrise Time column until he reaches the end of the table in his moon phases record. If he took all the numbers he calculated and wrote on the separate sheet of paper, then found their average, he would find that the moon rises (on average) about fifty minutes later every day.

Next, have your child examine the Moonset Time column. Ask him if he observes that the moon sets later every day just like it rose later every day. Ask him to calculate the number of minutes the moon sets later every day, and write down that number on another separate sheet of paper. Make the same calculation for the entire fourth column in his moon phases record. If he took all those number of minutes and found their average, he would find that the moon sets (on average) about fifty minutes later every day.

The moon rises (and sets) about fifty minutes later every day due to the moon's rotation about Earth. If the moon didn't rotate around Earth, then it would always rise and set at a fixed time every day.

MOON NAVIGATION

Before modern times a skilled navigator was a prized person in society. Navigation was accomplished using objects in the sky—the sun, moon, planets, and stars. Notable to those fine navigators were the movements of those objects in the sky. The canopy overhead that we call the sky was like a map that helped people find their orientation in space while also helping them tell time.

How can you use the moon to navigate through space and time? It all boils down to understanding the phases of the moon as the moon moves around Earth.

Everything in the sky rises in the east and sets in the west. That basic reality is a consequence of the earth's rotation. The moon is the closest celestial object to Earth, and it moves around the earth. It takes the moon about 29–30 days to complete one cycle around the earth. Because of this gradual rotation of the moon around Earth, the moonrise time (and moonset time) occurs later every day for each moon cycle.

New Moon Phase

At the beginning of a moon cycle, the moon is lined up in the same direction as the sun relative to an observer on Earth. In other words, if an observer on Earth faces the direction of the sun, the moon will be in that same direction as well. The moon is said to be in a new moon phase when it's in the same direction as the sun relative to Earth. In this phase, both the moon and sun rise above the horizon at the same time. They also set below the horizon at the same time. This means that a new moon *rises in the east at sunrise*, and *sets in the west at sunset*. Also, because the moon and sun in this phase are in the same direction relative to someone on Earth, the side of the moon that's lit by the sun is facing away from

Earth. This makes the new moon not visible on that day because the side of it that is lit is facing away from Earth.

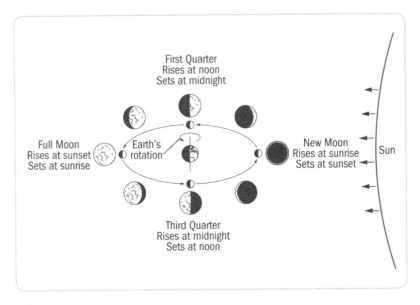

First Quarter Phase

At a quarter of the way through the moon's cycle, the moon is said to be in a first quarter phase. For an observer on Earth, this is when the *right* half of the moon's disk appears lit. A first quarter moon *rises in the east at noon*, and *sets in the west at midnight*. The first quarter moon is exactly halfway between a new moon and a full moon. Note that its rising time at noon is halfway between sunrise and sunset, and its setting time at midnight is halfway between sunset and sunrise.

Full Moon Phase

Half a moon cycle later, when the moon is on the opposite side of the sun (relative to an observer on Earth), the moon is said to be in a full moon phase. In this phase, when the sun sets the moon rises, and vice versa. This means that a full moon *rises in the east at* sunset, and *sets in the west at sunrise*. Because the lit face of the full moon that's facing the sun is also facing the earth, the entire disk of the moon is fully illuminated on that day.

Third Quarter Phase

At three-quarters of the way through the moon's cycle, the moon is said to be in a third quarter phase. This is when the *left* half of the moon's disk appears lit for an observer on Earth. A third quarter moon *rises in the east at midnight*, and *sets in the west at noon*. The third quarter moon is exactly halfway between a full moon and the next new moon. Note that its rising time at midnight is halfway between sunset and sunrise, and its setting time at noon is halfway between sunrise and sunset. Note that reference to rising and setting times at noon and midnight are approximate, not exact. Those times change slightly from season to season. They also move forward by one hour when daylight savings is added.

Astronomer

Astronomy includes the study of planets, moons, asteroids, comets, stars, galaxies, nebulae, dark matter, and everything pertaining to the universe. Astronomers focus on specific areas of study. Examples include solar astronomy, planetary science, evolution of galaxies, and the origin and evolution of stars.

Theoretical astronomers focus on developing computer models of the phenomena they are studying in order to understand its evolution in time. An example is creating simulation models that allow astronomers to understand the physical processes that underlie a star's physical appearance. Observational astronomers focus on collecting data by using a telescope—or sometimes a spacecraft—and analyzing their findings to test theories or answer questions. Most astronomers work in research in universities, though others work at aeronautics companies or agencies such as NASA.

The previous four phases are the main four phases of the moon on its cycle around Earth. If you place them on the perimeter of a circle, they would be separated from each other by a quarter of the circle's circumference. But what about the moon's phases in between these four primary phases? The following two paragraphs introduce the "in-between" phases.

The Waxing Journey

When the moon is in the first week of its cycle, a crescent moon is visible in the sky with its horns facing the left side of an observer. This crescent moon appears thicker night after night, and is known as a *waxing crescent moon*. In its second week, the moon no longer has a crescent shape; it starts to gradually become more and more rounded on the left side. In this second week of the moon's cycle (after the first quarter) it is known as a *waxing gibbous moon*.

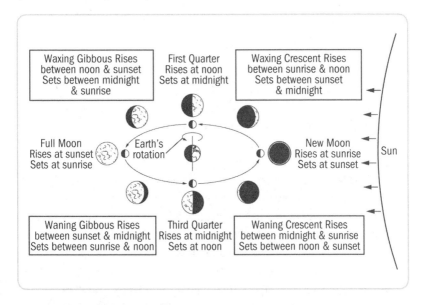

The Waning Journey

Once the moon is past its full moon phase, it is at the beginning of the third week of its cycle (before the third quarter). The moon is still rounded on both sides, but now the illuminated right side seems to get less and less rounded day after day. This is known as a *waning gibbous moon*. In the last week of its cycle, the moon's lit face becomes a crescent shape, but its horns are facing the right side of an observer. This crescent moon appears thinner night after night, and is known as a *waning crescent moon*.

The moon's motion in the sky is like a clock that's always been there. With this knowledge of the phases of the moon, and their rising and setting times, you and your child can now learn how to navigate using it. Make sure to study the phases of the moon with your child before you start using the moon to navigate.

MATERIALS NEEDED:
- Moon phases chart previously provided (with the main four phases)
- Red flashlight (for use during night observations)

PROCEDURE:
1. On a *full moon* night, step outside with your child right after sunset and look at the moon. Ask your child the following question: If the full moon rises at sunset, which direction are you looking at? Ask her if the full moon will be visible all night (since it just rose).
2. On the day of a *third quarter moon*, when the moon's disk is half-illuminated on the left, step outside with your child an hour before noon and look at the moon. Which direction are you both looking at when you see it? Remind your child that a third quarter moon sets around noon. Ask your child if this third quarter moon will be visible for the rest of the day into the evening.
3. A day *after a new moon*, when there is a thin crescent moon in the sky, step outside with your child right after sunset and look at the moon. Which direction do you both have to look at in order to see the crescent moon? Is it in the

direction the sun is setting? Ask your child if this crescent moon will be visible all night.

4. On the day of a *first quarter moon*, when the moon's disk is half-illuminated on the right, step outside with your child an hour after noon and look at the first quarter moon. In which direction are you both looking when you see it? Remind your child that a first quarter moon rises around noon. Ask your child if this first quarter moon will be visible for the rest of the day into the evening.

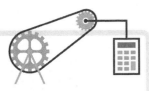

STEM Q&A

Why does the full moon appear bigger near the horizon?

This phenomenon is called the Moon Illusion. It's been known since ancient times, but has no real answer. In the early eleventh century, Ibn al-Haytham provided an explanation for the Moon Illusion. The apparent change in the moon is a psychological illusion because the mind perceives the moon as a closer object when it is near the horizon and "interprets" the moon as seemingly bigger. When the moon is higher in the sky, there are no objects around it (like trees) to compare it to, and so it feels more distant and seems smaller.

If your child's answer pertaining to the first question about the *full moon* was that she would look east because the full moon rises in the east (as everything else does), then she's correct. And if she said the full moon will be visible all night because it just rose at sunset, then she nailed it.

Examine your answers to the questions related to observing the *third quarter moon*. If you said you found the third quarter moon in the west because it was about to set at noon, then you're correct. And if your child figured out that this moon will not be visible for the rest of the day and into the evening because once it sets it disappears from the sky, then she's really beginning to tune into the moon phases.

You guessed right if you said you're looking west when observing a thin crescent moon, right after sunset, *the day after a new moon*. And yes, that moon was found in the same direction in which the sun was setting. And if your child said that the crescent moon will not be visible all night because it would shortly set in the west, then she's got it.

Finally, examine your answers to the questions related to observing the *first quarter moon*. If you said you found the first quarter moon in the east because it just rose at noon, then you're on target. Your child has most likely figured out by now that this moon will be visible for the rest of the day and into the evening, because it has just risen and will be visible for the next twelve hours.

Astrophysicist

While astronomers are concerned with measuring the positions and properties of celestial objects, astrophysicists focus on applying physics to astronomy in order to understand these objects.

Astrophysicists are also found doing research in universities as well as at places like NASA. However, an astrophysicist is mostly interested in the physics of celestial phenomena. For example, an astronomer may be interested in observing a black hole in some region in space and documenting its location in space. An astrophysicist would be involved in mathematically calculating how massive a star must be in order for it to become a black hole. Astrophysicists heavily use physics laws, including those in relativity, nuclear and particle physics, thermodynamics, and electromagnetism.

THE EASIEST CONSTELLATIONS TO RECOGNIZE

It's fun to look up at the sky and take notice of stars and the patterns they make. It's something that people have done throughout the world and throughout time.

Observed star patterns haven't changed their shape throughout millennia. When the ancient Greeks looked up at the sky, they perceived the patterns, as did the Babylonians and the Egyptians before them. The ancient Greeks gave a few names, based on their mythological figures, to the star patterns that were visible in the Northern Hemisphere. These star patterns, also known as *constellations*, still hold the names of many of the ancient Greek mythological figures today.

There are 88 known constellations throughout the Northern and Southern Hemispheres. This lesson will focus on four well-known and easily recognizable constellations in the Northern Hemisphere. You can observe some of these constellations throughout the year, but others only during certain seasons.

MATERIALS NEEDED:
- Compass
- Sky chart that shows the outline of some of the well-known constellations
- Red flashlight

PROCEDURE:
1. On your sky chart, identify with your child the shape of the star pattern known as the Big Dipper (which is part of the constellation Ursa Major). The Big Dipper has the shape of a

ladle that's easy to spot. Also, its stars are bright enough to see even with a little bit of light pollution.

2. Step outside in early August, around 9–10 P.M. Help your child find the direction north, using the compass. Looking over the northwestern horizon, gaze up gradually until you both find the Big Dipper.

3. The next constellation to help your child locate on the sky chart is Orion. Orion is easy to identify, starting with the three stars that are lined up diagonally close together. These three stars make up what is known as the belt of Orion (a legendary hunter from Greek mythology). The best time to observe Orion is in the winter. In fact, Orion is visible all winter long. To easily find Orion, have your child look for it above the east-southeast horizon around 9 P.M. sometime in early December.

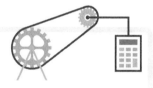

STEM Q&A

What's the meaning of these constellations' names?

Some of the constellations were named after characters in ancient Greek mythological stories. For example, Ursa Major was the big bear, Orion was a giant hunter, Cygnus meant "swan," and Cassiopeia referred to a queen, the wife of king Cepheus. Each one of these names was part of an elaborate mythological story that left its imprint on the night sky.

4. The next constellation to help your child locate on the sky chart is Cygnus. Cygnus is easy to identify because its stars make the shape of a cross. In fact, Cygnus is known as the Northern Cross. The best time to observe Cygnus is in late summer, in late August or early September. Have your child look high in the sky, almost overhead, around 9–10 P.M. in late summer, and try to identify the stars that make a cross pattern.

5. The last constellation to help your child locate on the sky map is Cassiopeia. Cassiopeia is easy to identify because it looks like a W or M. Cassiopeia never sets; the constellation is always above the horizon all year round. Such a constellation is called a *circumpolar constellation*. Pick a time to observe Cassiopeia, say in late October. Have your child look above the northeastern horizon at around 8–9 P.M. in late October, until he identifies the stars that make a W pattern.

Once your child learns to identify these constellations, have him trace how they change their position in the sky night after night. For example, by late April, Orion would have drifted westward far enough that it would have gone out of view below the horizon. Most of the Big Dipper is visible year round, and so is Cassiopeia. However, Cygnus would be totally out of view by winter, as it also would have drifted westward and disappeared below the horizon.

Identifying constellations is always a fun activity, especially when taking a walk or traveling by car at night. The next time you're on a night trip in the car, you can help pass the time by asking your child which constellations he can identify.

Biophysicist

A biophysicist is concerned with the study of life on every level, from the smallest level of atoms and molecules to cells and organisms to the environment surrounding them.

Research in biophysics helped reveal the double helix structure of DNA. Biophysicists identified the locations and functions of all the genes in human beings, and some of the genes in more than 100,000 species. Biophysicists explore using microorganisms to generate biofuel, to clean water, and to create new drugs.

CHAPTER 4

OTHER EARTH SCIENCES

Rocks and soil are part of the makeup of our planet Earth, in addition to water on the surface and under the ground. All of that is engulfed by a vast atmosphere that makes it possible for life to exist.

The sciences related to Earth surround us. You've always had a direct experience of them when you've gone to a swimming pool and played with a ball and watched it float in the water. And every time you've tuned in to the evening news to hear the forecast, you've heard the science of our planet splashed all over that forecast.

This chapter will help you and your child explore some important concepts pertaining to earth science that affect your everyday life. It will also feature some of the professions related to this fascinating area of science.

NORTH VERSUS SOUTH POLE

The terms *north pole* and *south pole* usually make people think of the geographic regions known as the North Pole and the South Pole. There are, however, two other kinds of north and south poles. Those are the north magnetic and the south magnetic poles. And when referring to our planet, we should be specific about whether we're referring to the north *geographic* or the north *magnetic* pole.

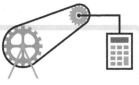

STEM Q&A

What are the geographic north and south poles?

The north geographic pole lies in the Arctic and is the most northern point on Earth. The south geographic pole lies in the Antarctic and is Earth's most southern point. Planet Earth rotates about itself once every day. It spins about an imaginary axis that connects the north and south geographic poles.

How do magnetic poles behave near each other? When you use a compass needle to find north, does the magnetized compass needle point in the direction of Earth's north magnetic or the south magnetic pole? And how are the earth's *magnetic* poles related to the earth's *geographic* poles?

MATERIALS NEEDED:
- 1 sewing needle
- 2 flat metal-head straight sewing pins
- Strong bar magnet
- Compass

PROCEDURE:

1. If the bar magnet sides are not labeled N (for North) and S (for South), then have your child use the compass needle to identify N and S. Have her bring one side of the bar magnet near the side of the compass needle that's labeled N (it is usually the side that's colored in red). If the N side of the compass needle is attracted to the side of the magnet she brought near it, then that side of the magnet is S (South). Tell your child to make a note of which side of the magnet is S.

2. Ask your child to sit at a table and to place one of the straight pins to her left and the other one to her right.

3. Tell your child to hold the head of the needle in one hand.

4. Now have her hold the bar magnet in the other hand.

5. Ask your child to stroke the needle, from head to tip, with the *north* side of the bar magnet. Have her do this repeatedly in the same direction at a steady, medium speed about 5–10 times, then set the needle somewhere in front of her, away from the two pins. While holding the head of the pin to her left, ask your child to stroke the pin, from head to tip, in the same fashion with the *north* side of the magnet, then place the pin back on the table to her left.

6. Now tell your child to pick up the needle by its head, and bring its *tip* very close to the *tip of the left pin* (which is lying on the table). What happens? Does the tip of the needle repel or attract the tip of the left pin? You should observe the needle's tip and the left pin's tip repelling each other, as illustrated in the following diagram. This is because both needle and left pin were magnetized from head to tip by the same *north* magnetic pole. This makes the needle and left pin magnetized identically. In other words, if the tip of the

needle became magnetized north, the tip of the left pin was also magnetized north.

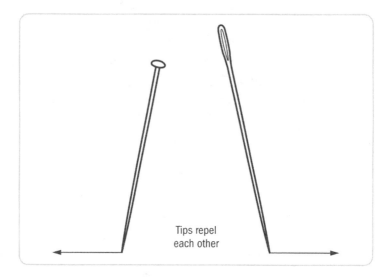

Tips repel each other

7. Now have your child do the following. While holding its head, ask your child to now stroke the right pin, from head to tip, with the *south* side of the magnet in the same fashion as before. Have her place the pin back on the table to her right.

8. Now have your child pick up the needle by its head, and this time bring its *tip* very close to the *head of the right pin* (which is lying on the table). What happens? Does the tip of the needle repel or attract the head of the right pin?

You should observe the needle's tip and the right pin's head repelling each other, as illustrated in the following diagram. This is because the needle was magnetized by the *north* magnetic pole (making its tip magnetized *north*) while the right pin was magnetized by the *south* magnetic pole (making its tip magnetized *south*). Note that when one side of the needle becomes magnetized *north* (for example, its tip), then its head automatically becomes magnetized *south*. The same is true for the pin: When its tip is magnetized *north*, then its head is automatically magnetized *south* and vice versa. That's just how nature works!

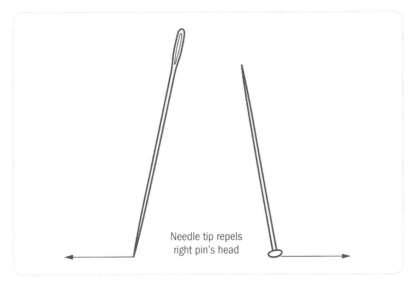

Needle tip repels
right pin's head

Ask your child what was different between the left and right pins. Remind your child that the left pin's tip was magnetized north. What was different about the way she magnetized the right pin?

Your child probably remembered that when magnetizing the right pin, the magnet was flipped, and therefore the left and right pins were magnetized by opposite magnetic poles. This would cause the poles on the right needle to be the reverse of the poles on the left needle, as illustrated in the diagram to the right.

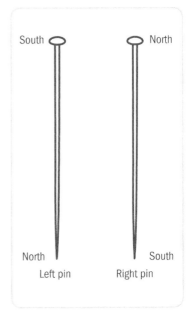

Now ask your child this question: Why did the left pin's tip repel the needle's tip, while the right pin's head did the repelling?

STEM Q&A

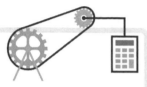

Where are the north and south magnetic poles located?

Earth's north and south magnetic poles are not permanent, as the geographic poles are. The north-south magnetic poles on planet Earth flip every few hundred thousand years, making the north magnetic pole a south one, and vice versa. Scientists discovered this when studying the ocean floor of the Mid-Atlantic Ridge, which has stored this pattern over millions of years.

Your child most likely found out by now that *magnetic poles that are alike repel*. She most likely remembered that the needle's tip was magnetized north, as shown in the diagram. That's why the needle's north tip repelled the left pin's tip (which was also magnetized north). The same needle's tip later repelled the right pin's head (also magnetized north).

If magnetic poles that are alike repel, what about magnetic poles that are opposite? Ask your child what she thinks. If her answer is

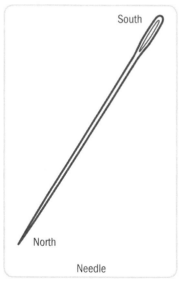

Needle

that they *attract*, she's correct. This means a magnetic north pole attracts a magnetic south pole, and vice versa.

People use a compass to find the geographic north direction. It's an especially handy tool when hiking in the wilderness. A compass needle is very much like the sewing needle your child magnetized. The red side of the compass needle is magnetized north, while the other side of the needle is magnetized south. So here's an interesting question to ask your child: In which geographic direction would Earth's south *magnetic* pole be? Is it in the direction of the *geographic* north pole, or the *geographic* south pole? Remind her that a magnetic north is attracted to a magnetic south.

Since the magnetic north pole of the compass needle points toward the geographic north, then it must have been attracted by a magnetic south pole, therefore the *geographic north* pole must be the *magnetic south pole*.

Geologist

A geologist studies all the materials that make up Earth. This includes solids, liquids, and the surface layers as well as the interior of Earth. They study volcanoes, earthquakes, landslides, faults, and floods. This gives them the ability to survey land for safe building. Geologists are concerned with long-term changes in the land and in the climate.

Geologists are involved in many other types of investigations. Some geologists survey land for natural resources such as water, oil, and natural gas, as well as examine methods to extract them. Based on their observations of rocks and fossils, a geologist can describe the geological processes Earth underwent for the past several million years.

ACTIVITY:

PRESSURE, TEMPERATURE, AND THE WEATHER

If you've ever been in a crowd of people trying to exit a place very quickly (such as when there is an emergency), you know about pressure. You might also know that it feels hotter when there are so many people pushing through a door or a gate. This is exactly how the air molecules "feel" when the pressure is high: The heat is turned on (the temperature goes up). Pressure is the amount of force applied to a surface area.

But what happens when the pressure is low? Does the temperature go down?

MATERIALS NEEDED:
- Balloons (have several handy in case one pops)
- Freezer
- Video device to document the event (optional)

PROCEDURE:
1. Ask your child to inflate a balloon using his own breath. Make sure he inflates it to a point where the balloon is stretched to the limit without popping. (You might need to do this more than once if the balloon pops.)
2. Place the balloon on an empty rack in the freezer for at least 24 hours.
3. Remove the balloon from the freezer. If you are making a video, start recording the balloon before you remove it from the freezer. What do you observe?

Does the balloon look different than when you first placed it in the freezer? Does it look smaller and wrinkly? What begins to happen to it the instant you pull it out of the freezer and into the warmer environment of your kitchen? Does the balloon begin to expand back to its previous size?

If you've recorded the entire event, you can replay that video rather than place the balloon back in the freezer for another 24 hours to see the effect again.

In order to understand the relationship between temperature and pressure, you need to zoom down to the level of the air molecules inside the balloon.

molecules

A molecule is made of two or more atoms (the smallest building blocks in nature). For example, an oxygen molecule is made of two oxygen atoms that are bonded together. When you breathe in oxygen, you are breathing oxygen molecules. A water molecule is made of one oxygen atom bonded with two hydrogen atoms.

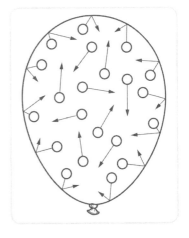

You can think of the air molecules as little balls constantly moving and bouncing off each other. They also bounce off the inside wall of the balloon. The arrows in the drawing show the motion of the air molecules. When those molecules bounce off the walls of the balloon, they apply pressure to it.

What does it mean to apply pressure? When you press against a surface, you apply pressure. For example, if you stand on a trampoline, you're applying pressure (or force) to the surface of the trampoline. You can see the effect of that pressure on the trampoline because its surface stretches down.

Similarly, the air molecules press against the balloon surface as they bounce off it. This pressure makes the balloon stretch out.

Meteorologist

A meteorologist is someone who observes Earth's atmospheric phenomena, then analyzes and explains these phenomena using scientific methods and principles. A meteorologist can also forecast effects in Earth's atmosphere and how these effects relate to life on our planet. Meteorologists are mostly known for predicting the weather and climate, and its impact on our lives.

A meteorologist can hold a variety of different jobs: the "weather forecaster," giving the daily weather forecast; an atmospheric researcher; a college professor; or an employee in a private meteorological company or with the government.

Once inside the freezer, the air inside the balloon cools down. When the air is cooler, its molecules don't move around and bounce as much. They slow down and get closer to one another. In a way, they're like you when you're cold: You want to move less and cuddle close to someone. Notice how the arrows in the drawing get smaller, showing a slower motion of the air molecules. They're not bouncing as hard off each other and off the balloon surface. This makes the balloon less inflated.

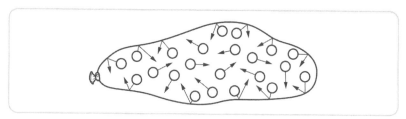

This means that when the temperature of the air goes down, so does its pressure. When cooler air moves in, it's usually accompanied by low pressure.

WHY DO SOME THINGS FLOAT?

When you throw a rock into the water, it sinks. But huge, heavy objects like ships float in water as they travel the oceans. Why is that?

It's all about buoyancy. What is buoyancy and what factors affect it?

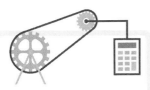

STEM Q&A

Who was the first scientist to understand buoyancy?

Archimedes was a Greek scientist who lived in the third century B.C. He was the first scientist to understand buoyancy and how to apply it to real-life dilemmas that required solutions. For example, using his understanding of buoyancy, Archimedes was able to detect that the king's crown was not made of pure gold, but was mixed with a cheaper metal such as silver.

When an object is placed in a fluid such as water, the object is pushed up by a force from within the water called the *buoyancy force*. There's more than one factor that makes the buoyancy force larger or smaller. One such factor you can investigate is the surface area with which the object touches the fluid. The following experiment will help your child specifically explore the relationship between the buoyancy force and the surface area of an object placed in water.

MATERIALS NEEDED:

- Aluminum foil roll
- Big plastic tub 14" (L) × 14" (W) × 6" (H)
- Vise grip
- Pliers
- Scissors

PROCEDURE:

1. Using scissors, cut 2 sheets of aluminum foil that are 12" × 7".

2. Assist your child in filling the tub about ¾ full with water.

3. Give your child 1 of the aluminum foil sheets. Carefully help her place the flat sheet on top of the water. Take caution not to bend the sheet so that you don't let any water float on top of the sheet. What do you both observe?

4. Now let your child crumple the second aluminum sheet into the tiniest ball she can make. Then, using the vise grip and the pliers, assist her in squeezing the aluminum foil ball down to an even tinier ball. Keep squeezing it until it becomes a small ball with a diameter of no more than ½".

5. Place the ball of crumpled aluminum on top of the water. What do you observe?

Did the aluminum sheet float? What about the aluminum ball? Did it sink? Why do you suppose they behaved differently even though they're made of the same material (aluminum foil)? Ask your child what the difference is between the flat and the crumpled aluminum foil. Remind her that they were identical to start with; they were the same size and are made of the same stuff. Does she think it matters that the flat sheet has a larger surface than the crumpled one?

If she guesses yes to that last question, she's absolutely right. The crumpled aluminum ball sinks straight to the bottom of the tub. The flat sheet, with its larger surface area, floats on top of the water.

Take a few moments to consider and discuss how the water influences the flat sheet as it floats on top of it. The water pushes up on every part of the sheet's surface. This is the buoyancy force. The larger the sheet's surface the water can push against, the more *distributed* the force is over that surface (as shown in the picture) and the larger the buoyancy force.

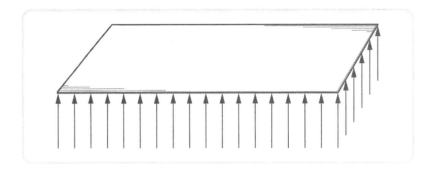

When the aluminum foil is crumpled to the size of a small ball, the water can only push up against a tiny, tiny surface area. The smaller the surface the water can push against, the smaller the buoyancy force.

As long as the upward buoyancy force on an object is equal to the weight of the object, it will float. That's exactly why ships have a large surface area. The buoyancy force pushing the ship up—so it can stay at the surface—must be just as big as the weight of the ship, or else it would sink.

Hydrologist

Hydrologists study the water on our planet, how it moves across the surface of Earth, its quality, and its availability as a resource. They find solutions to issues concerning water supply to cities and farms. When there are problems with water pollution, hydrologists are involved in cleaning up and preventing future pollution to such water resources.

Hydrologists are often found in the field collecting water samples. They perform analyses on those samples in order to check the quality of the water. In addition to testing water quality, hydrologists engage in a variety of other tasks, such as working on flood control near rivers and designing proper underground disposal of hazardous waste.

ACTIVITY:
BALLOONS, SPOONS, AND DENSITY

When you throw a penny in the water, it sinks. But when you throw in a twig, it floats. Even if the wood is much larger than the penny—say a log—the wooden log still floats. Why is that?

It's all about the density of the material you're using. Density is a measure of how much mass (matter) is compacted into a specific volume of the material. Since mass is measured in grams (g) and volume is measured in cubic centimeters (cm^3), density is measured in grams per cubic centimeter (g/cm^3).

One way you might test the density of materials is by squeezing them. If one material takes more effort to compress than another, it's denser. For example, a metal toolbox is far denser than a loaf of bread.

Is there a more scientific way to test the density of material rather than trying to squish it? Here's the bottom line for the method of measuring density: When you attempt to place an object in a cup full of water, depending on the object's density, it'll spill more or less water. This phenomenon happens because everything occupies a certain amount of space. The water in the cup occupies the entire space inside the cup. If you attempt to add more things into that space, some of the water has to spill, or become displaced.

You'll be measuring mass in this activity. Mass is a measure of how much matter is in an object. Mass is measured in grams, the abbreviation for which is g.

MATERIALS NEEDED:
- Several different-sized rocks (a size that fits in your fist, some slightly smaller, some slightly larger)
- Child's rubber duck
- Electronic kitchen scale (with a "grams" setting available)

- Bucket
- Plastic tub the bucket can easily fit into
- 2 measuring containers or glasses
- Water hose connected to a faucet
- Pencil and paper

PROCEDURE:

1. Ask your child to place the kitchen scale on a flat surface, then turn it on. Make sure the scale is set to the "grams" setting. Make sure to tare (reset to zero) the scale properly.
2. Have your child place the rubber duck onto the scale. Ask her to record, in grams, the mass of the duck on her paper—for example, 25 g.
3. Have your child place each of the rocks on the scale one by one, measuring and recording the mass of each one of them, also in grams.
4. Ask your child to choose the rock that has a mass close to that of the rubber duck. Have her set the other rocks aside so she doesn't accidentally use them.
5. Have your child place the bucket into the plastic tub, and place the tub on the ground. Using the water hose, your child can now fill the bucket with water to the very top. You can assist her in filling the bucket so that no water spills out of it. It is important that the water reaches the very top of the bucket, to the point just before it spills.
6. Ask your child to drop the chosen rock into the bucket. Ask her to observe whether the water spills out of the bucket. Assist your child in emptying the spilled water from the tub into one of the measuring containers.
7. Pull the rock out and place the bucket back into the tub, then refill the bucket to the very top without overfilling it.
8. Have your child take the rubber duck and submerge it totally into the bucket by pushing it down with her hand just far enough to where the duck's head is just below the surface

of the water. Ask her to observe whether the water spills out of the bucket into the tub. Empty the spilled water from the tub into one of the measuring containers.

Was there water that spilled out when the rock went into the bucket? What about when the rubber duck was submerged? Check the two water levels in the two measuring containers. Was it the same amount of water in both cases? Which one displaced more water out of the bucket, the rock or rubber duck?

Your child most likely figured out that the rubber duck displaces far more water than the rock. The rubber duck has a mass similar to a rock, so it must be something else about the rubber duck that made more water spill. Ask your child what she thinks is different about the rubber duck than the rock. Is it perhaps the material it is made of? Is it possibly its size (volume)?

If she guessed yes to either of those two questions, she guessed right. Discuss with your child the answer to the first question. The duck is made of rubber, but the rock is made of a material called silicates. Rubber isn't as dense as rock; the density of rock is much greater than that of rubber. The greater the density, the more matter is compacted into the object. The density of the rubber in the duck is about 0.5 g/cm^3, while the density of rock is well over 2 g/cm^3.

Now discuss with your child the answer to the second question, the one pertaining to the size of the two objects. Because the densities of rubber and rock are different, the sizes (volumes) of the rubber duck and the rock have to be much different in order for their masses to be the same. Recall that you had your child pick the rock that measured closest in mass to the duck, using the kitchen scale. The greater the density of an object is, the smaller its size. The rock has a much greater density; that's why its size is smaller than the rubber duck.

Since the size of the duck is larger than the rock, it would need to displace more water if it's going to sit in the space inside the bucket. Stated differently, the rubber duck takes up a lot more space than the rock does. So when you submerge the duck, it has to move more water out in order to make room for itself. The rock doesn't need to move as much water out.

The denser an object is, the less water it displaces when it is submerged compared to an object with lesser density but equal mass.

So why does a penny sink in water when a wooden log floats? When a material has density greater than that of water, it sinks. Copper's density is almost 9 g/cm^3, much greater than the density of water. When a material has density less than the density of water, it floats. The density of most wood is under 1 g/cm^3.

You can test the density of other things compared to water. Drop a spoon in the water bucket. If it sinks, its density is greater than water's density. Drop an inflated balloon in the water bucket. You will find that it floats on top of the water. That's because the air inside the balloon (if you discount the thin walls of the balloon) is much less dense than water. The density of air is very close to zero (0.001225 g/cm^3)!

THE PHYSICS OF FLOATING FEATHERS

If you've ever dropped a feather, you've noticed that it seems to float or sway in the air as it falls to the ground. Most other objects, such as books and toys and keys, don't behave the same way when dropped. Why do feathers appear to float or sway when many other objects don't?

To answer this question, it's first necessary to understand the concept of a force. When you push on a box, you're using a force. When you pull on the string of a kite, or when you lift up a cup of water, or when you blow bubbles using your breath, you're using a force.

Another example of a force is the force of gravity. Earth pulls on all objects with a downward force—that's the force of gravity. Your child can test the existence of the force of gravity by holding a pencil in her hand and letting go of it. The force of gravity pulls the pencil straight down.

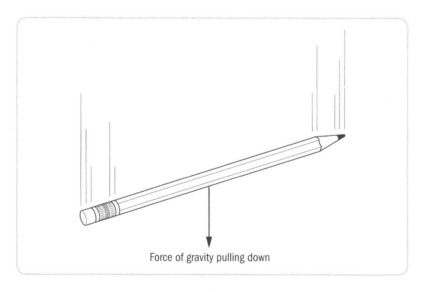

Force of gravity pulling down

Consider what happens to another object—say a box resting on the floor—when you exert a force on it by pushing it. If the box is initially at rest, it begins to move and gains velocity. When the box goes from not moving to moving, its velocity changes. When any object goes from not moving to moving, physicists say it *accelerates*. In other words, the object's velocity *changes*; it goes from having no velocity to having some velocity. Therefore, it can be said that *acceleration* is the *change* in velocity.

STEM Words to Know

velocity

Velocity is a measurement of both the speed of an object and the direction it is moving in. A moving object has velocity. A nonmoving object has no velocity. When a car is moving at 60 mph, that number is referring to how fast the car is moving, or the car's speed. However, when you say the car is moving at 60 mph heading north, you are reporting both how *fast* as well as the *direction* the car is moving. You are reporting velocity.

Sometimes people confuse the concept of velocity with the concept of momentum. Velocity of an object has to do with how fast it's moving. *Momentum* is related not only to how fast the object is moving, but also to how massive the object is. A truck moving at 60 mph has a lot more momentum than a car moving at 60 mph because the truck has a greater mass.

What caused the box, or the pencil, to accelerate? According to Newton's second law, the force of the push (on the box), or the force of gravity (on the pencil) causes the object to change its velocity, or to accelerate.

A simple experiment will shed light on the reason feathers sway or seem to float as they fall toward the ground, while objects like pencils don't. Instead of using feathers, you can use something easier to find around the house.

MATERIALS NEEDED:

- 2 sheets of 8½" × 11" paper

PROCEDURE:

1. Give your child one of the sheets of paper. Have him hold it horizontally about 4 feet above the ground, then let go. Observe how the flat sheet of paper sways, or appears to float, as it falls toward the ground.
2. Now take the other sheet of paper, have him crumple it into the tiniest ball he can, hold it about 4 feet above the ground, and let go. What did you both observe?

Did the crumpled sheet of paper fall to the ground in the same manner as the flat sheet? Why do you suppose they behaved differently, even though they're made of the same material (paper)?

Here's a hint: Ask your child what the difference is between the flat sheet and the crumpled sheet of paper. Remind him that they were identical to start with, and they're both made of the same material. Do you think it matters that the flat sheet has a larger surface than the crumpled one?

If he answered yes to that last question, he's absolutely right. It does indeed matter that the flat sheet has a larger surface than the crumpled sheet. The crumpled sheet of paper falls straight to the ground—no sway whatsoever. The flat sheet, with its larger surface area, sways or "floats" as it's falling to the ground.

Take a few moments to consider and discuss the forces influencing the flat sheet as it falls. It's already been established that the force of gravity pulls the sheet down. However, while the sheet is falling through the air, another force comes into play. This other force is the force of the air that pushes upward against every part of the paper's surface. It's the very same force that pushes up on a skydiver's parachute. If the surface of the flat sheet is larger, the air can push up more. This force that involves the air pushing upwardly is called *air resistance*.

If you look at the two forces acting on the sheet of paper (shown in the following diagram), you'll notice that the two forces are acting in opposite directions.

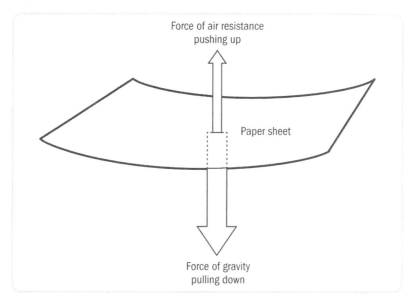

Force of air resistance
pushing up

Paper sheet

Force of gravity
pulling down

Seismologist

Seismologists are considered earth scientists. They study seismic waves that propagate through geological material. This material includes the interior of our planet all the way to the core, as well as the surface crust.

Through analyzing data from earthquakes, seismologists are able to infer the structure of our planet's interior. Seismologists may also advise companies that are exploring for oil. (Digging for petroleum often involves explosions that cause seismic waves.) Seismologists also work with engineers to assess methods to minimize damage from earthquakes to buildings and other manmade structures. This allows for construction standards to be improved.

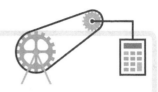

How does Newton's second law work if there is more than one force?

In tug of war, the object getting pulled is the rope. It's being pulled to the right and to the left at the same time, so it is experiencing two opposite forces. If the rope is pulled with equal forces from both sides, it doesn't move. But if one team—say the team on the right—pulls slightly harder, then there is a difference between the two pulls. The difference between the two opposing forces is small and points in the favor of the direction of the bigger force (to the right). That difference is what causes the team on the right to begin accelerating—to change their velocity from not moving to moving. The bigger the difference between the two opposing forces, the bigger the acceleration and the faster the change in velocity.

When you're playing tug of war, if one team pulls *slightly* harder than the other, that team will make everyone begin to move in their direction *slowly*. It's exactly the same with the two opposite forces of gravity and air resistance. When the force of gravity is *slightly* bigger than the force of air resistance, the object's velocity changes in the direction of the bigger force *slowly*—that is, the flat sheet sways, or seems to float, as it falls to the ground. The same principle applies to a falling feather.

When you crumple the sheet of paper, the surface area the air can push against becomes smaller, reducing the force of air resistance. With the crumpled sheet, the force of gravity is *much* bigger than the force of air resistance, and it will pull harder, making the crumpled paper fall to the ground *faster*. This is also why a pencil falls straight to the ground when it's dropped instead of swaying or floating like a feather.

WHAT'S IN SOIL?

If you've looked at dirt across the landscape in many places, you've probably noticed that dirt comes in many colors. Soil can have a strong brown color, or a dark gray, reddish yellow, red, or even black color. The different colors of soil tell an expert soil scientist about the chemical composition of that soil. Let's explore some basic interpretations about soil color, and see what chemical elements in the soil are responsible for those dominant colors.

MATERIALS NEEDED:
- Notebook to record observations
- Pen

PROCEDURE:
1. Go outside into your backyard or drive to a park where you can directly observe soil that's not covered with grass or other landscaping material such as mulch or rocks. If there is greenery or other cover that prevents you from seeing the soil, you can dig out some of the dirt to view it.
2. Once you've accessed the soil and you're able to observe it, ask your child what color the soil is. It might be easier to give your child a list of possible colors to help her make the distinction. Ask her if the soil is dark, light, or red.
3. Tell your child to record her observations in her notebook.
4. Drive to a garden nursery where they sell plants and dirt for your garden. This is a good place to look at different color dirt that might be available at your local nursery. Once you arrive, ask your child to observe the color of the dirt in the piles available. Have her record those colors in her notebook.

5. If you live in or near the countryside, drive around in early spring or late fall and observe the soil colors in those fields. Have your child record those soil colors as well.

6. Finally, if you have access to hiking trails with natural surroundings, take your child for a hike and have her bring her notebook. Ask your child if she notices new colors in the soil on the sides of the trail. Ask her to record those colors.

Soil Scientist

Soil scientists evaluate soils. They are able to analyze data related to soil in order to understand the resources present in soil. This is especially important for agricultural purposes since soil is a natural resource. Some of the activities soil scientists engage in include evaluating forest soils and wetlands. They should also be able to investigate soil that would be used for waste, including the disposal of residential waste.

A soil scientist is knowledgeable about the soil's chemistry, physics, and biology. For example, a soil scientist is able to study the stability of the soil, its ability to drain or retain moisture, and its sustainability and impact on the environment.

Now it's time for your child to examine her observations. Did your child discover several colors to the different soils she observed? Assist her with learning the interpretation of the different colors of soil she observed. Soil that is light in color or looks whitish is rich in calcium and magnesium carbonates, or some other salts:

- **Calcium** is one of the chemical elements in the periodic table of the elements, which lists all elements known to us in the universe. Calcium is grouped with alkaline earth metals, and it has a soft gray color in appearance. Calcium is an important element for living organisms, and it is essential for the mineralization process of teeth, bone, and shells.

- **Calcium Carbonate** is a chemical compound that has calcium and carbon. It also has oxygen. It's white in color, and it's known by other names, such as limestone. It's a main component in rocks, shells, pearls, and even eggs.
- **Magnesium Carbonate** is a chemical compound that has magnesium and carbon, as well as oxygen. It's also white in color. Like calcium, magnesium is an element in the periodic table. It's also grouped with alkaline earth metals, but has a shiny gray color. Magnesium carbonate is found, for example, in natural unrefined salt, such as Himalayan salt.

If the soil is dark or black, there's a lot of organic matter in it such as the breakdown of residual plants. Sometimes the dark soil points to the presence of charcoal in it. Red soil indicates the presence of iron in it.

Oceanographer

Oceanographers deal with many disciplines, including marine life, ocean circulation, ecosystems, ocean floors, and plate tectonics. Biological oceanographers study plants, animals, and organisms that live in the marine environment. A chemical oceanographer studies the ocean water, its composition and cycles, and its interaction with the seafloor as well as the atmosphere. Physical oceanographers study physical processes in the ocean, such as waves and currents, the transport of sand to and from shores, and the erosion of coastlines. A geological oceanographer studies the ocean floor—its mountains, valleys, and ridges.

If you and your child encounter soil of other colors besides the ones listed above, then have her do a search online for the chemical composition of that soil color.

CHAPTER 5
CHEMISTRY

Chemical reactions happen inside human bodies all the time. That's how food is broken down inside the stomach in order to digest it, and that's how the body makes heat to stay alive, among many other processes that constantly take place inside a human body. But chemistry is also everywhere around us. An appetizing brownie can't be so tasty without a whole lot of chemistry taking place within the ingredients. It's certain chemicals in foods that make them taste sour, sweet, or salty. Some serious chemistry is also going on inside the batteries that power all the electronic devices society has come to rely on these days.

This chapter will explore some basic ideas in chemistry and give you and your child a peek at how chemistry is such an integral part of your daily lives.

HOW BATTERIES WORK

You use batteries in many things every single day of your life. You charge the battery of your phone every day; your alarm clock may have backup batteries in case the electricity goes out; your rechargeable laptop and tablet are convenient because you can carry them around. The watch on your wrist and even your car require battery power to run.

How does a basic battery work? What happens inside a battery so that it can provide power? What's necessary to make the battery work? Why does it eventually stop working so that you have to buy a new one? The best way to learn about batteries is by making one at home.

MATERIALS NEEDED:

- 5 zinc washers, size #10
- 5 pennies
- Freshly squeezed lemon juice
- Thick paper towel
- Scissors
- Plate
- 2 electric wires with alligator clips at their ends
- Piece of aluminum foil (3"–4" in width)
- 1 LED light bulb

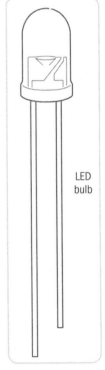

LED
bulb

PROCEDURE:

1. Assist your child in cutting the paper towel into square pieces that are 2" × 2". Tell him to cut up about 10 such pieces.
2. Now have your child fold each paper towel piece in half 4 times. In other words, fold

the 2" × 2" square in half, making a 2" × 1" rectangle. Then fold that rectangle in half, making a 1" × 1" square. Repeat the last two steps again until the final folded piece would be a thick square with sides that are ½" × ½" that are slightly smaller than the penny's diameter. Have your child fold all the 2" × 2" paper towel pieces in this fashion before moving on to the next step.

3. Have your child immerse the folded pieces of paper towel into the freshly squeezed lemon juice, without squeezing out the juice. Ask him to place those pieces on the plate.

4. Have your child clip 1 alligator clip wire to 1 arm of the LED bulb, and another wire to the other arm.

5. Next, ask your child to place one of the zinc washers on the aluminum foil. On top of the washer, have him place one of the folded paper towels soaked in lemon juice, then a penny on top. Have him place another folded paper towel that's soaked in lemon juice on the penny, then a zinc washer on top of that. Basically have him alternate between washer and penny (with folded paper towels soaked in lemon juice in between penny and washer) until the last piece on top is the fifth penny. Tell him he doesn't need a paper towel over the last penny. Now he's got a battery.

6. It's time for your child to test his battery. Tell him to touch the loose end of one of the alligator clip wires to the aluminum foil. Assist him in touching the other alligator clip wire's loose end to the top penny. What do you observe? Does the LED bulb light up?

When the LED bulb lights up, tell your child it is totally powered by the pennies, zinc washers, and lemon juice!

A battery requires three ingredients: a zinc electrode, a copper electrode, and a liquid containing electrolytes, such as the lemon juice. An electrode is a metal used in an electric circuit that comes in contact with some other nonmetal part of the circuit (such as an electrolyte). Copper has a stronger electronegativity than zinc does, which means copper has a stronger ability to attract electrons than zinc does. In this case, zinc gives away electrons that flow toward the copper (via the wires), and the bulb lights up.

Chemical Engineer

Chemical engineers apply principles of chemistry, physics, and biology in solving problems that relate to food, fuel, drugs, and other chemicals. They design the processes for testing chemical compounds, as well as the instruments they use for such testing.

For the most part, chemical engineers work in laboratories. Depending who they work for, they might have to spend time in refineries, industrial plants, processing plants for food, or some other location. This allows them to collect data to analyze later in their office or laboratory. Some of their jobs include improving processing techniques for food, or developing methods to mass-produce foods or drugs in order to make them more affordable, or designing more efficient procedures to refine different petroleum products.

Because the zinc gives up electrons to copper, the zinc electrode is the negative terminal of the battery (also known as the *anode*). And because the copper is eager to receive electrons from the zinc, the copper electrode is the positive terminal of the battery (also known as the *cathode*).

But what role does the electrolyte play inside the battery? It's specifically the acid inside the lemon juice that acts as an electrolyte and dissociates into positive and negative ions. A simple example of an electrolyte is table salt. It consists of one sodium atom and one chlorine atom that are combined. When table salt is dissolved in water, the sodium and chlorine atoms dissociate, becoming positive and negative ions. The negative ions from the electrolyte allow the zinc atoms that just lost electrons (and became positive as a result of that) to move away from the zinc electrode. The positive ions in the electrolyte move toward the copper electrode, because they like the newly arriving electrons the copper took from the zinc, and they will snatch those electrons.

An animated picture looks like this: When the zinc gives away electrons, the electrons fly away along the path of the wire toward the copper that's electron-thirsty. The wire connecting zinc to copper acts like a superhighway for the electrons. The ions inside the electrolyte are heavy, and don't move around as easily as the lighter electrons can along the superhighway. However, the negative ions can sweep away (neutralize) the zinc that lost its electrons. If the negative ions didn't do that, then there would be too many zinc atoms that lost electrons congregating around the zinc electrode, and the flow of electrons would stop. The positive ions are bribed by the newly arriving electrons on the copper electrode, and move toward the copper.

STEM Words to Know

electronegativity

Metal atoms, like zinc and copper, have a tendency to either lose some of their electrons or attract other electrons. When a metal atom has a strong tendency to attract electrons from other atoms, it is said to have a strong *electronegativity*. Copper has a stronger electronegativity than zinc.

So the zinc and copper electrodes on their own can't make up a battery. Neither does the electrolyte on its own. The lemon juice alone, or the lemon itself, is not a battery. To turn a lemon into a battery, you need the zinc and copper electrodes. In place of a lemon you can use a lime, a potato, or anything that contains acid, such as vinegar.

Eventually all the zinc gets used up. Also, when all the negative and positive ions in the electrolyte find partners on either electrode, the electrolyte no longer exists. Whichever one happens first brings the life of the battery to an end.

Analytical Chemist

Analytical chemists deal with matter. They analyze its structure and determine its composition. They do their work to make sure food, water, and pharmaceutical drugs meet quality standards for consumption, and are compliant with regulations. They decide which samples to isolate and preserve, and then test them.

Analytical chemists can work in government jobs or can be employed by academic institutions or industrial companies. In addition to doing chemical analyses, they invent new methods for measurement, and design the instruments required for them. They can also be found working in law offices and in marketing firms.

ACTIVITY:

ALKALINE OR ACIDIC?

One of the many ways food can be categorized is by whether it's *alkaline* or *acidic*. Whether a particular food is considered alkaline or acidic depends on a measurement of certain ions in that food.

In order to understand the nature of ions, we must start with a discussion on atoms. An atom is the smallest building block in nature. The smallest atom found in nature is the hydrogen atom. A hydrogen atom (whose symbol is H) is made up of one proton (a positive charge in the center—or nucleus—of the atom) and one electron (a negative charge that moves around the nucleus). One positive charge attracts one negative charge; therefore, if the hydrogen atom has one positive charge and one negative charge, it is electrically neutral. Most atoms can easily share electrons with other atoms; when they do, so that all the combined atoms are electrically neutral, they form what is known as a *compound*.

Atoms can lose or gain electrons. When a neutral hydrogen atom, H, loses an electron, it is left with only one positive charge (or proton), but no electrons; it is then called a hydrogen ion (and gets the symbol H^+). An ion is not electrically neutral. Remember that atoms can combine together; they do so by sharing electrons. A hydrogen atom, H, can share one electron, while an oxygen atom, O, can share two electrons. If a neutral oxygen atom, O, shares one electron with a neutral hydrogen atom,

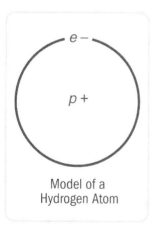

Model of a
Hydrogen Atom

H, there is still another electron the oxygen atom can share in that union. Such a union between one hydrogen atom and one oxygen atom produces an ion known as a hydroxide ion, OH^-.

What do ions have to do with a food substance being acidic or alkaline? If the substance has a high concentration of hydrogen ions, H^+, it's considered acidic. An acid is a chemical compound that turns litmus paper red

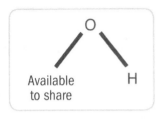

because its pH is low. It usually tastes sour. Acids have the ability to react with some metal compounds. For example, the acetic acid found in vinegar can react with calcium carbonate (found in eggshells), forming bubbles of carbon dioxide gas.

However, if the substance has a high concentration of hydroxide ions, OH^-, the substance is considered alkaline. The measurement of acidity or alkalinity is called a *pH measurement*. To measure the pH of a substance is to measure the concentration of hydrogen ions in it. In fact, the letters pH refer to the "power of hydrogen."

The numerical measurement of pH ranges from 0 to 14. At pH=0, the substance is strongly acidic, and at pH=14, the substance is strongly alkaline. Pure water has pH=7 (neutral pH). Therefore, any substance that has a pH less than 7 is considered acidic, and if its pH is higher than 7 it is alkaline. For example, white vinegar has a pH range between 2 and 2.4, making it acidic. Milk has a pH of about 6.6, making it closer to neutral. Baking soda has a pH that is slightly higher than 8, making it alkaline.

What about other foods you have in your kitchen? Are they acidic or alkaline? You can easily measure the pH of any liquid food using litmus paper.

Obtain some litmus paper and test the pH of the following foods. (Consult the chart that comes with your litmus paper to establish what color changes indicate acids and alkalines.) It's best to test these foods in a liquid form, so **juice a fruit or vegetable before you test it**. Record your results in the following table. Also, feel free to add more food items to the list. For example, find out what happens to the pH of your milk once you add a sugar-rich cereal to it. NOTE: Use freshly squeezed fruits and vegetables.

RECORD OF FOOD PH

Food (in liquid form)	pH value	Acid, Alkaline, or Neutral
Club soda		
Cow's milk		
Coconut milk		
White vinegar		
Apple cider vinegar		
Sugar in spring water		
Salt in spring water		
Carrot		
Cucumber		
Tomato		
Lemon		
Orange		
Pineapple		
Bell pepper		
Sweet potato		
Eggplant		
Buttermilk		
Sugar-sweetened fruit juice		

Different foods have an acidifying or an alkalizing effect once in the human body. If you would like to find out how different foods affect the body in terms of pH, read the next section, The pH of Foods.

Biochemist

Biochemistry combines both chemistry and biology. Biochemists explore chemical principles and processes within living organisms. For example, they investigate viruses and bacteria, but also more complex life forms such as animals and human beings. They analyze structures on the level of molecules when studying them.

Biochemists can be found working in pharmaceutical companies, developing and testing new drugs. They also work in hospitals. They may conduct tests on blood samples and explore possible new treatments for diseases. When they work in the agricultural industry, they may genetically engineer new plants that can grow fast and are resistant to diseases.

THE PH OF FOODS

Most people move through their everyday lives without thinking about whether the food they eat is alkaline or acidic. In fact, most people think of the measure of acidity, or the pH test, as something that belongs in a chemistry lab. You might be among the few who do test the pH of the food you eat. But another important question to ask is the following: Does the pH of food change when it's in your body? In other words, does the pH of food assimilated in the body test differently than if you test the pH of that food outside the body?

You might recall that the numerical measurement of pH ranges from 0 to 14. A strongly acidic substance has pH=0, while a strongly alkaline substance has pH=14. Pure water sits right in the middle at pH=7 (neutral pH). If a substance has a pH less than 7, it is acidic. If its pH is higher than 7, it is alkaline. For example, our stomach acids have a pH range between 1 and 3. That number can increase to 4–5 when there is food in the stomach. The small intestines, however, have a pH that is equal to 8, making the environment in the small intestines alkaline. It is very important for your blood to have a pH range from 7.35 to 7.45, otherwise, it can be fatal.

In order to test the pH effect of food once you ingest it, use pH strips that have a pH range from 4.5–9.0 to test your saliva. Such strips come in small increments (smaller than one, usually increments of a half) allowing for more accuracy in readings. Also, those strips usually come with a color chart you can use to read the pH based on the color. Make sure to juice a fruit or vegetable before using it. Record your results in the following table. Feel free to add more food items to the list of things you would like to test.

MATERIALS NEEDED:

- pH testing strips ranging from 4.5 to 9.0
- Cow's milk
- Coconut milk
- Vinegar
- Sugar in spring water (2 tablespoons of sugar in an 8-ounce glass of water)
- Spring water
- Carrot
- Cucumber
- Tomato
- Lemon
- Orange
- Sugar-sweetened fruit juice

NOTE: Make sure you use the fruit and vegetable items when they are freshly squeezed.

PROCEDURE:

1. Prepare your child by telling her that she can only test one item on the list at a time. No food or drink other than water should be taken at least 2 hours before testing the pH of the saliva. Otherwise the readings would not be accurate. Perhaps it's best to test a couple of items every day.

2. Have your child do this experiment first thing in the morning, before eating anything, even before brushing her teeth (the toothpaste can affect the measurement). Have her prepare the pH strip and the food she wants to test (in liquid form), then rinse her mouth with plain spring water.

3. Next, tell her to touch one of the pH strips on her tongue, and immediately match her strip colors to the chart in order to identify her base pH value before putting any food in her mouth. Have her record that pH value on the table.

4. Immediately after the previous step, have your child swish around in her mouth about 1 ounce of the liquid food she plans on testing that day in its pure form, then swallow it.

5. Have your child wait 2 minutes before testing her saliva. Have her use a new pH strip to test her saliva after the liquid food she just ingested. Ask her to touch a new pH strip

to her tongue and immediately match the new strip colors to the chart. Once she identifies the pH value of her saliva after ingesting this food, have her record that value in the third column on the following table.

6. Ask your child the following questions: Did this food make her saliva more acidic or more alkaline? In other words, did her pH shift slightly toward becoming a little more acidic or more alkaline? Was this food acidifying or alkalizing? Have her record her answer in the last column of the table.

RECORD OF FOOD PH			
Food (in liquid form)	pH before ingesting the food	pH after ingesting the food	Acidifying or Alkalizing?
Cow's milk			
Coconut milk			
Vinegar			
Sugar in spring water			
Carrot			
Cucumber			
Tomato			
Lemon			
Orange			
Sugar-sweetened fruit juice			

Through this activity, hopefully your child will gain some insight into how different foods can change the chemistry of her body. It's often surprising to find out that lemons have an alkalizing effect on the body once ingested, even though lemons test as an acid when they're outside the body. It all depends on how the food is chemically assimilated in the body.

Pharmacologist

Pharmacologists are concerned with studying the effects of chemicals and pharmaceutical drugs on cells. They study these responses in human and animal cells. The main concern of a pharmacologist is not just developing new drugs, but making sure they are safe to use, and measuring the correct doses to administer.

Pharmacologists design experiments to test drugs. They may also carry out clinical trials to test the newly formulated drugs on humans. They collect data, then analyze it. This allows them to find the harmful effects of the drugs in order to explore ways to minimize or eliminate them. Pharmacologists often work in teams with other research scientists.

SEPARATING SALT FROM WATER

Table salt is a common presence in most modern diets. Food without a proper amount of salt just doesn't taste the same. Before electricity was invented, when people didn't have refrigerators, meat was cured with salt in order to preserve it over a long period of time.

But where does salt come from? Is it grown on trees? Of course not. It comes from salty bodies of water. But salt doesn't have to come from deep within the ocean; it's fairly easy to remove salt from seawater. Ancient people did it thousands of years ago, so the process doesn't require much technology. In fact, you can even try it at home.

MATERIALS NEEDED:
- Salt (unless you live near an ocean and have access to saltwater from the ocean)
- Water
- Large Teflon pan
- Teakettle, or cooking pot

PROCEDURE:
1. If you're using ocean water, have your child pour half a gallon of ocean water into the Teflon pan. It's best to do this experiment in the summer when it's hot, otherwise the salt will take a long time to be extracted. (If you are using ocean water, skip the next two steps.)
2. If you don't have access to ocean water, then warm up half a gallon (8 cups) of water in the teakettle or pot, and pour it into the Teflon pan.
3. Ask your child to add ½ cup of table salt into the warm water, and stir it until all the salt has dissolved.
4. Have your child place the Teflon pan outside in a sunny place, where it can get sun for a good portion of the day. If

she's doing this experiment indoors, have her place the pan in front of a window that gets a lot of sun. Inform your child that she'll have to be very patient, as it may take days for the water to evaporate from the pan and leave the salt behind.

5. Remind your child to check on her pan every day, so she can observe the changes. What does she find after all the water has evaporated? Is it a whitish powder?

The powder left behind after the water evaporates is salt. Salt is a chemical compound that's composed of one sodium atom and one chlorine atom. The name of this compound is sodium chloride. In the periodic table of the elements, sodium has the symbol Na, and chlorine has the symbol Cl, so sodium chloride would be chemically expressed as NaCl. When salt is dissolved in water, the sodium dissociates from the chlorine, forming ions. The sodium becomes a positive ion, Na^+, while the chlorine becomes a negative ion, Cl^-. The reason salt dissolves in water is because the positive sodium ions (Na^+) are attracted to the negative side of the water molecules, while the negative chlorine ions (Cl^-) are attracted to the positive side of the water molecules.

STEM Words to Know

periodic table of the elements

The periodic table of the elements organizes all 118 known atoms in a big grid. Starting at the top left corner of the table, hydrogen is listed as the lightest of all atoms. Moving from left to right along each row, each atom gets heavier by one proton than the one before it. The elements are arranged in certain locations, depending on specific characteristics of each. The modern periodic table traces its roots back to Russian chemist Dmitri Mendeleev. Mendeleev classified the 63 elements known by 1871 according to certain patterns he noticed. He used his table to predict properties of more elements that were discovered later.

If you had to mix salt with water to make saltwater, then the white powder is the table salt you used, which is sodium chloride (NaCl). If you used ocean water, then that powder may have more than just sodium chloride. There may be other minerals present in the ocean water that are now part of your salt. If you obtained the ocean water from an area where the ocean is clean and not polluted, you can use the salt you just made.

On average, 1 gallon of ocean water would give you a little more than ½ cup of salt. So if you live near an ocean and you want to have locally made salt, you can't get more local than right in your own home.

Toxicologist

Toxicologists are concerned with studying the harmful effects of chemical compounds on the cells in living organisms. We live in a world that is highly saturated with chemical hazards such as pesticides, air pollutants, and other chemicals in the water we drink. This makes the work of toxicologists extremely important to our health and well-being.

Toxicologists develop better methods to test the biochemical effects of exposure to certain chemical material that may cause diseases. They may work in industries such as cosmetics, food, drugs, and agricultural products. They may also work in the public service to establish safety regulations for such products.

ICE VERSUS DRY ICE

You've probably seen, or at least heard of, dry ice. It's said that dry ice can keep things much cooler than ice made from water. You might have even been to a Halloween party where someone used dry ice to make eerie floating fog.

Now you'll get a chance to investigate the difference between regular ice and dry ice. What is "dry" about dry ice? Doesn't all ice get wet when it begins to melt?

MATERIALS NEEDED:
- 1 bag of dry ice
- Insulated gloves for handling dry ice
- Container to put the dry ice in
- 2 small bowls
- Spoon
- 2–3 ice cubes from the freezer
- 2 different color balloons

PROCEDURE:
1. Have your child put a few cubes of ice from the freezer into one of the bowls.
2. Using the insulted gloves, assist your child in placing the dry ice into a container. *Caution:* always use insulated gloves when handling dry ice. Place a small chunk of dry ice into one of the small bowls.
3. You'll probably have to wait a while until the ice from your freezer starts melting in the bowl. But check out the bowl of dry ice. What do you notice? If you wait long enough for the ice from the freezer to totally melt in the bowl (an hour or two), what's left in that bowl?

4. Use the insulated gloves again. Stretch open the neck of one of the balloons, and have your child to use a spoon to scoop up some of the dry ice and drop it into the open mouth of the balloon. Tie the balloon shut and set it on your counter.
5. Have your child place a couple of ice cubes from your freezer into the other balloon, then tie it shut and set it on the counter close to the balloon with dry ice.
6. Wait a while until the ice from your freezer starts melting. When you come back to check out the ice in each of the balloons, how do you find each balloon? Do you find both of them still at the same size as when you tied and left them on the counter?

When you came back to check the two bowls of ice, you probably found one with water from the melted ice cubes, while the other one was empty! Where did the dry ice go? Did it evaporate? Actually, yes. Dry ice undergoes *sublimation* rather than evaporation. Some substances go directly from being a solid to a gas, without passing through a liquid state. When this happens, it is said the substance has undergone sublimation. Frozen carbon dioxide (dry ice) is one such example.

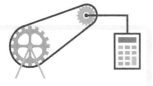

STEM Q&A

What is the difference between evaporation and sublimation?

A substance like water can go from being a solid (ice) to a liquid (water) then to a gas (water vapor) when the water evaporates. When a substance goes through the intermediate liquid state as it transitions from a solid to a gas, then it is said that the liquid undergoes evaporation as it turns into gas. When a substance undergoes sublimation, it goes directly from a solid to a gas without ever becoming a liquid in between.

But what about the two balloons? The one with regular ice just ended up having water in it once the ice melted. The one with dry ice ended up being inflated! Why is that? Well, when water is frozen, it occupies roughly a similar size as (or just slightly larger than) liquid water. That's why that balloon stays about the same size. However, the balloon with dry ice gets bigger because the dry ice underwent sublimation, turning from a solid into a gas. Dry ice is none other than frozen carbon dioxide gas, like the gas you expel from your lungs every time you exhale. Gases expand to take up a lot more space than solids do, because gases are much less compacted than solids. Gases have a much lower density than solids. That's why the balloon inflates.

The temperature of water when it freezes is 32°F, while the temperature of dry ice is about –109°F! That's why you should use insulated gloves when handling dry ice. Otherwise you can get a freeze burn.

Lab Technician

Lab technicians in chemistry work alongside chemical engineers and chemists to assist them in testing chemical material. They use laboratory equipment to conduct experiments often designed for research and development. They may set up lab equipment, prepare chemical solutions, perform chemical experiments, collect and analyze data, and write reports to present their findings.

The work of chemistry lab technicians is always in a laboratory, whether they work in industry, in an academic setting, or in any other institution. Most jobs for chemical lab technicians require a two-year associate degree. They receive their training at the job site.

CHAPTER 6

BIOLOGY

Biology is the study of life and living organisms, including humans, animals, plants, and other organisms such as fungi, bacteria, and algae. In particular, biology focuses on studying the growth of these living organisms, how they populate, and how they function in order to survive.

Plants are in every person's landscape—in your backyard, in a nearby park, or simply planted alongside the roads. Bacteria and fungi populate the world around us, as well as the world within our bodies. Every living thing produces offspring to make sure their species continue on.

In this chapter, you and your child will explore some basic concepts in the biology of plants, fungi, and humans, such as some of the functions that enable them to survive and some characteristics they pass down from generation to generation. Through these explorations, biology will "come to life" in your living environment. In addition, you'll learn about some of the exciting vocations in the biological sciences.

ACTIVITY:
HOW PLANTS MAKE FOOD: PHOTOSYNTHESIS

Every living organism needs to eat. Some are picky eaters; others are not. Plants in general are among the least picky eaters. The presence of forests that are not maintained by anyone shows that those plants are not finicky about their nutritional needs.

Plants use a process called *photosynthesis* to make their own foods in the form of sugars. Photosynthesis is a chemical process that can only occur within the biological systems of living plants. In this chemical process, the plant stores the energy of sunlight inside sugar molecules it makes from water and carbon dioxide molecules. It takes six water molecules plus six carbon dioxide molecules (plus sunlight) to make one sugar molecule and six oxygen molecules. Plants make their own sugars using only sunlight, water, and carbon dioxide, which is present in the air humans and animals expel from their lungs when they exhale. Plants take human waste gas products (carbon dioxide) and use it to make their own food.

The amount of sunlight a plant is exposed to has an effect on how much "food" it can make for its own growth. There's an easy way to observe how sunlight directly affects a plant's ability to make food for itself so it can grow.

MATERIALS NEEDED:
- Organic cotton wool
- Approximately 15 mustard seeds
- Spray bottle
- 2 deep glass or ceramic plates

PROCEDURE:

1. It's best to do this experiment during a warm season. Have your child make a thick layer of cotton wool in both plates, then slightly spray each with water to dampen the cotton.

2. Now ask your child to sprinkle some of the mustard seeds on each of the cotton surfaces. Have her spray the seeds with water again until the cotton wool is lightly soaked with water and the seeds are wet on top.

3. Have your child place one of the plates in a dark corner of the house that doesn't get sunlight at all, and the other plate near a window that gets plenty of sunlight throughout the day without being in direct sunlight.

4. Have your child check the moisture of the cotton wool in both plates every day. If she's doing this experiment in the summer, she might want to spray the plate in the lit spot once in the morning and once in the evening to make sure the seeds don't get dry.

5. Have her check and see if her seeds are sprouting in the first ten days. Once they do, have her observe how fast those sprouts grow in the plate that gets sunlight compared to the one that doesn't. Ask her if there's a difference in the sprouting speed in both plates.

6. Urge your child to look after her two plates and touch the cotton wool on each to check for dampness every day. In about 30 days there should be a full canopy of mustard greens on at least one of them. Which one has the full canopy of greens?

7. Encourage your child to continue to spray both plates with water and to keep the cotton wool damp on each for another ten to fifteen days. Which plate has its mustard greens grow taller?

If your child reports back to you that the mustard greens in the plate near the window that gets sunlight experienced the fastest growth, she now understands how critical sunlight is to the plants' growth.

Everything grows when it eats and gets nutrients. The way plants make food for themselves using sunlight, water, and carbon dioxide through the photosynthesis process involves something in their green leaves called *chlorophyll*. The molecules of chlorophyll are found in every green plant, and it's what makes plants and algae look green. These molecules absorb sunlight and use the energy that reaches them from the sun to make (or synthesize) sugars from basic ingredients like water and carbon dioxide. This entire process the chlorophyll molecules perform is what's called photosynthesis. The chlorophyll molecules can synthesize sugars (food for the plant) by using sunlight. That's where the name *photo* (meaning light) and *synthesis* (indicating that it is making something) comes from.

Botanist

Botanists are plant scientists. They study the plants' organisms as well as their interaction with their surrounding environment. They may also conduct experiments on plants to investigate how they grow and survive under different conditions.

A botanist may be concerned with studying the large, naked-eye characteristics of plants, or may be interested in looking through microscopes at the plants' cellular level. Botanists may also be interested in studying processes that take place on the molecular level, such as photosynthesis. They may be interested in conservation, such as focusing on conserving native plant species against the invasion of non-native plants.

All the energy in the sunlight absorbed by the plant is stored inside the sugar for later use. One interesting result from photosynthesis is that plants release the oxygen freed through the process back into the air. As the plant uses carbon dioxide and water coupled with sunlight, it not only makes sugar inside its own "body" but also releases oxygen as a result of that process. This is why there's a concern about losing more trees and forests on Earth. The plants "breathe out" oxygen for humans and animals to survive, so a reduction in that oxygen source is cause for concern.

Ecologist

Ecology is a science that is concerned with the relationship between living organisms such as plants and animals and the environments in which they live. Ecologists specialize in certain types of environments. For example, marine ecologists work with plants and animals that live in seas and oceans.

Ecologists may study environmental pollutants that affect the life and reproduction of living organisms. They also study the consequences of human activities on the environment. They may be found working at sites where pollution is taking place—for example, at chemical and oil spills in rivers and seas.

ACTIVITY:
DECIDUOUS VERSUS EVERGREEN TREES

Depending on where you live, you may see trees that lose their leaves for part of the year and become "naked," trees that keep their leaves yearlong, or a combination of both. This behavior in a tree is part of the tree's scheme to survive in the environment in which it lives.

In general, trees are categorized in two ways with respect to whether they lose or keep their leaves throughout the year: *deciduous* and *evergreen* trees. Deciduous trees lose all their leaves during certain parts of the year, while evergreen trees keep their leaf coverage year round. Most trees with needle-leaves, which are members of a family of trees known as coniferous trees, are evergreen trees.

STEM Q&A

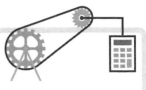

Are there other deciduous plants besides trees?

Yes. Any plants that lose their leaves during certain parts of the year are called deciduous. This includes shrubs and herbaceous perennial plants that live for several years. Examples include mint and basil as herbaceous plants, while lavender and Russian sage are considered shrubby perennials.

Your child would learn a great deal about the natural world in his immediate environment by creating an inventory of the trees in your area. With a few specific observational tools he might grow fond of studying trees and plants.

MATERIALS NEEDED:

- Time to walk in your neighborhood
- Time to walk in a nearby park
- Time to walk in a state park
- Small notebook to keep observations

PROCEDURE:

1. This is an activity that may span the length of two seasons starting with summer. Take a walk with your child with the intent to study the trees in your neighborhood. Help him become familiarized with the different shapes of the mature trees on the first walk. Tell him to notice the shapes of the trees. Are they round or cone-shaped, or some other shape? Remind him to record his observations in his notebook at the end of the walk. You might want to encourage him to draw a sketch or take a photo of each tree so he can remember them later.

2. The second time you go for a walk, ask him to notice the shapes of the leaves on the different trees he identified the first time. Ask him to specifically notice if the surfaces of the leaves are wide and big, or narrow and small. You can prompt him to collect a leaf sample if the tree is near the sidewalk. Remind him to record these additional observations in his notebook when he's done. Encourage him to sketch the outline of each leaf. This will help him assess how large or small the leaf size is.

3. As the days progress, help him become aware of which trees lose their leaves and which ones stay green. Remind him to record his observations in his notebook.

4. Do the same activities when you have a chance to visit a nearby park. In a park environment, your child has opportunities to observe more trees, and to collect more leaf samples for his sketches.

At the end of the fall season, you can go through your child's notebook with him to examine what information he has collected. You can help him organize his findings by asking him a few simple questions: How does the size of the leaves from trees that shed their leaves compare to those leaves from trees that didn't? In other words, was the leaf size of deciduous trees significantly different than the leaves of evergreen trees? Which ones were larger? Also, how did the shape of a deciduous tree compare to that of a evergreen tree? Encourage your child to look back through his notebook for answers to these questions.

Environmental Scientists and Environmental Engineers

Environmental scientists use their skills and knowledge in science to protect the environment, along with the health of human beings. They're often involved in the cleanup of polluted areas. They also play an important role in advising policymakers in creating new policies pertaining to the environment.

Many environmental engineers are employed in industry to help reduce pollutants and waste. When working in the field, they collect samples in order to analyze them in the laboratory. This allows them to make recommendations on reducing hazardous material produced during industrial processes.

If your child noticed that deciduous trees have leaves that are large in surface area compared to evergreen trees, then he's figured out one important clue to identifying which trees are deciduous or evergreen. Also, if he noticed that deciduous trees have a rounded shape on top, he now has two clues. Here's where you can assist him in putting it all together so he can see the bigger picture.

Deciduous trees require more nutrients in order to grow and survive. They do so by first growing broad leaves that can take in more sunlight. That's why their leaves are relatively larger than those of evergreen trees. The large leaves increase their photosynthetic abilities. They also maximize the amount of sunlight each leaf receives by having a round canopy on top. The roundness of the canopy allows more leaves to be exposed to sunlight. When the trees eventually shed their leaves and the leaves fall on top of their roots, the leaves break down and compost over time, enriching the soil with nutrients for the next growing season. These trees essentially produce their own fertilizer.

Such trees can't survive in an environment that's very harsh, where the soil is poor and water is scarce.

Marine Biologist

Marine biologists study all kinds of creatures that live in the seas and oceans. This includes fish such as sharks (for fishery biologists), mammals such as whales and dolphins (for marine mammalogists), and microscopic organisms such as plankton (for microbiologists).

Marine biologists are often engaged in research as well as education. This means they work in or with educational institutions such as universities, and also zoos and aquariums. They may also work on a body of water in which aquatic creatures live to ensure environmental standards free of pollutants. Marine biologists are employed by both the public and private sectors, and by both for-profit and nonprofit employers.

Evergreen trees work differently. Their leaves are very small compared to the leaves of deciduous trees. Their leaves can look needle-like, and aren't exposed to as much sunlight as the broader leaves of deciduous trees. This isn't a problem for evergreen trees because they keep their leaves year round, and so photosynthesis happens throughout the year. The needles on an evergreen tree don't all fall at one time because such trees don't need soils that are rich in nutrients. Evergreen trees don't require fertilizer in the way deciduous trees do; they're fine making just enough food from photosynthesis year round using their tiny leaves. Some evergreen trees' conical shape helps minimize damage by wind, ice, and snow.

There are more deciduous trees and forests in the eastern half of the country, where water is abundant and the soil is richer with nutrients. More evergreen trees are seen in the western half of the country, where the climate tends to be harsher and the soil poorer in quality. Examples of deciduous trees are oak, maple, mulberry, black walnut, birch, and elm. Some examples of evergreen trees include pine, firs, spruce, and junipers.

FERMENTATION: MAKING SOURDOUGH STARTER

Bread has been an essential staple for human beings for thousands of years. The most commonly consumed bread today relies on a very important biological process called *fermentation*. Fermentation is a chemical process that involves microorganisms such as yeast or bacteria. The fermentation process converts sugars and carbohydrates into alcohol, releasing carbon dioxide gas.

Fermentation doesn't only occur during the process of making bread; other examples of fermentation happen during the process of making wine and beer. Fermentation is also occurring when milk becomes yogurt.

Is it possible to observe the process of fermentation? When bread rises as the dough sits in a warm place, it seems difficult to notice fermentation happening. There is the before-and-after effect, where the dough seems to have doubled in size. But is there a more direct way to "see" the fermentation process release carbon dioxide gas?

MATERIALS NEEDED:
- All-purpose, unbleached wheat flour
- Spring water
- Wide-mouth 16-ounce glass jar
- Cotton cheesecloth
- Wide rubber band
- Spoon

PROCEDURE:

1. It's best to do this experiment in a warm season. Have your child place 5 tablespoons of all-purpose, unbleached wheat flour in the glass jar.

2. Now tell her to stir just enough spring water into the flour to make it the same consistency as pancake batter. Ask her to add the water gradually, stirring it into the flour. Assist her in gauging whether the consistency is like pancake batter, or if more water is needed. If the mix turns out too watery, tell her she can add a little more flour to fix it.

3. Help your child to cut a piece of the cheesecloth to cover the top of the jar with some excess extending past the rim of the jar. You might want to tell your child that the cloth is used to cover the jar instead of a jar lid in order to allow the mix to "breathe."

4. Now have your child secure the cheesecloth around the rim of the jar with a wide rubber band. Have her place the jar in a warm room, but not in direct sunlight.

5. Inform your child that she'll need to stir the mixture with a spoon once a day for several days in order to prevent mold from forming on the surface.

6. After about two days (depending on the temperature of the room in which the jar sits) have your child look closely at the contents of the jar. What does she observe? Are bubbles beginning to form?

7. Encourage your child to check on her jar every day and observe the changes happening inside of it. Are there even more bubbles forming every day?

8. When the bubbles start to make the batter rise in the jar, let your child know that it's time to "feed" those microorganisms inside the mix with a few more tablespoons of flour. Remind your child to also add a little more spring water. Tell her to add just enough water to keep the mix at the consistency of pancake batter.

9. Now have your child observe the contents of the jar closely, perhaps two or three times a day, in order to see the changes that will happen more quickly. Look for more bubbles in the mix. Ask your child if she observes how those bubbles make the mix rise inside the jar. When this happens, the starter mix is now ready to be used to make bread. A mix like this is called a *sourdough starter*.

This fermentation process is the ancient process people used to make bread for thousands of years. The reason the flour starts to undergo fermentation is because yeast is everywhere. This is the naturally occurring yeast that is present in the flour, in the air, on the skins of grapes and other fruits, etc. When the conditions are right—meaning when there is moisture and a warm environment, as well as "food" for the yeast in the form of sugars or carbohydrates—the yeast microorganisms start to "eat" those sugars and carbs, converting them into alcohol and carbon dioxide. It's the carbon dioxide gas that shows up as bubbles in the starter mix, making it rise. It's the active life cycle of those microorganisms that gives bread the ability to rise in order to have just the right texture.

Microbiologist

Microbiologists study microorganisms, including bacteria, algae, fungi, viruses, and parasites. This is a world too small to be observed with the naked eye, so microbiologists use microscopes to do their work. They investigate how these organisms multiply and how they interact with their environment.

Microbiologists' investigations include the harmful effects of microorganisms, such as viruses, and also their important functions that are essential to life, such as some bacteria, fungi, and algae. Microbiologists are found working in hospitals, medical schools, government laboratories, and in industry.

As long as you continue to "feed" the starter mix by adding more flour and water, it will survive. There are families who've kept their sourdough starter "alive" for hundreds of years, passing it down from generation to generation.

Every time you need to make sourdough bread, you can use part of the starter to make the bread rise, then "feed" what remains in the jar with 2–3 tablespoons of flour and some water to bring it back to the same consistency as it was before. You can look up recipes online for sourdough bread.

Biotechnologist

Biotechnologists work in a field that combines living organisms with technological application in order to make new products. Examples include designing organisms that can produce useful chemicals, such as antibiotics.

There's a wide range of vocations available for biotechnologists. They include the fields of medicine and agriculture, among others. Some biotechnologists may work on environmental applications. For example, a biotechnologist may work on developing microorganisms to treat polluted water, or may produce plastics that are biodegradable in order to preserve the environment.

POTATO, CARROT, AND CELL OSMOSIS

When you feel thirsty, you reach for a glass of fresh water. Because the human body is composed of 70 percent water, this liquid is very important in many functions of the body, down to the level of the cells. But how do the cells "drink" water once the water is made available around the cells? The answer lies in something called *osmosis*.

Osmosis is a natural, biological process that happens whenever there are two water-based liquids with different concentrations present on either side of a surface that is semipermeable. For example, when there's water with low salt content on one side of a semipermeable surface and highly salted water on the other side, some of the water from the low-salt side migrates and moves through the semipermeable surface into the high-salt side, until the concentration of salt on both sides becomes equal. It is specifically and only the *water* molecules that move from the low-salt side to the high-salt side in order for both solutions to reach equilibrium in salt content.

STEM Words to Know

semipermeable

A semipermeable surface is one that allows certain substances to pass through but not others. For example, plastic wrap is not permeable at all, while a cotton cloth is totally permeable, letting all liquids pass through. A biological semipermeable surface is a cell wall or membrane. It allows water (but not anything dissolved in the water) to pass through its surface.

In general, whenever something is dissolved in water, like salt or sugar, the dissolved substance is referred to as the *solute*, while the water is referred to as the *solvent*. Because water has a smaller molecule than the salt or sugar, the water molecules are the ones that move across the partially permeable (or semipermeable) surface.

But how does this work for cells of living things? Can the effects of osmosis be observed directly?

MATERIALS NEEDED:

- 1 potato
- Apple corer
- 1 large carrot
- Vegetable peeler
- Fresh water
- Salt
- 2 clear drinking glasses
- Tablespoon
- Two different color cotton strings, each 6" in length

PROCEDURE:

1. Assist your child in peeling the potato.
2. Use the apple corer to carve out a cylindrical piece of potato about 4" in length. This will take some effort, so you might want to assist your child in this process.
3. Have your child tie a piece of cotton string around the potato cylinder with a double knot, then slide it off the potato cylinder. Have your child save that loop of string to use for measuring the diameter of the potato cylinder later.
4. Fill one of the glasses with plain water and place the potato cylinder in the glass. You will be letting this piece sit in the glass for a few hours.
5. Now have your child use the other glass to prepare a very salty water solution. Ask her to fill the other glass with water,

then have her add 2–3 tablespoons of salt to the water. Stir the salt until it is all dissolved in the water.

6. Have your child peel the carrot. After that's done, tell your child to tie the other color cotton string around the widest part of the carrot with a double knot, then slide it off. Save that loop of string to use for measuring the diameter of the carrot later.

7. Now tell your child to place the carrot inside the second, salty glass of water with the wide side of the carrot on the bottom (for stability). Allow the carrot to sit in the salty water for a few hours as well.

8. A few hours later, have your child check on the potato cylinder. What has changed about it? Has it become fatter or more slender? Remind your child that she can use the string she tied around the potato cylinder earlier to measure. Does that tied string still fit around the potato cylinder after it has soaked in water?

9. Have your child check on the carrot a few hours later as well. What has changed about the carrot? Is it still crisp and hard, or has it wilted and become somewhat soft? Has it become fatter or more slender? Remind your child that she can use the string she tied around the carrot earlier to measure. Does that tied string still fit snugly around the widest part of the carrot after it has soaked in salty water?

If your child found that the potato had increased in diameter, then she has visibly seen the effects of osmosis on the cells of that potato. Additionally, if she found that the carrot became wilted and more slender and that the string now fits loosely, then she's seen the effects of osmosis on the carrot. Osmosis in the potato allowed water to move into the cells of the potato, and the potato became fatter. In the carrot, however, water moved *out* of the carrot cells and the carrot became thinner.

Imagine the wall of each cell inside the potato and carrot as a semipermeable membrane. On either side of the cell wall there is water (solvent). There are also many different substances that are dissolved in the water (solutes) inside the cell.

Zoologist

A zoologist loves to study everything about animals. They're passionate about the well-being of animals and like to educate the public about them. They identify certain animal species, document them, and observe these animals in the wild as well as in captivity.

Zoologists can also perform a wide range of jobs. They develop new veterinary medicines and test them. They work on identifying endangered species and habitats, and then conserving them. They do field as well as laboratory research. Zoologists also work in government agencies, as they develop new policies and regulations regarding wildlife.

When the concentration of the solutes inside the cell is high compared to the outside of the cell, water molecules move across the cell wall into the cell until the concentration of solutes is the same on both sides of that wall. This is why the potato cells inflate as water crosses the semipermeable wall into each cell. There's a higher solute concentration inside the cells than outside, and water moves from the low to the high solute concentration until there's equal concentration on either side of the cell membrane. This is how the cell "drinks."

When the concentration of the solutes outside the cell is high compared to the inside of the cell, water molecules move across the cell wall out of the cell until the concentration of solutes is the same on both sides. This is why the carrot cells deflate as water crosses the semipermeable wall out of each cell. There's a higher solute concentration outside the cells than inside, and water moves from the low to the high solute concentration until there's equal concentration on either side of the cell membrane. This is how cells lose water.

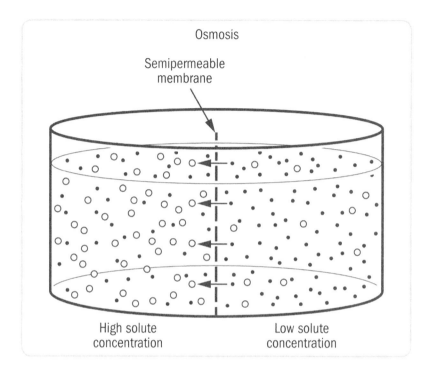

This same process takes place inside the human body. Osmosis allows water to move into the cells or out of them. In order for cells to "drink" water, there has to be a lower concentration of solutes (or higher concentration of water) outside the cells for water to move into the cells. This is partially why water is so important for all living organisms. So the next time you drink water, remember that your cells are also drinking that water.

DOMINANT VERSUS RECESSIVE TRAITS

It's often easy to identify which children belong to which parents at a school or daycare center. There are certain characteristics the children have that they've inherited from their parents. The parents' genes determine the children's genetics. Genetics is the study of hereditary traits, the differences and resemblances that get passed down from generation to generation in all living beings, humans, animals, plants, etc.

Genes are like a blueprint that carries instructions on how the child will look, among many other traits. Every child carries two sets of genes: one from the mother and one from the father.

Certain traits are determined by the set of genes one has inherited from both parents. One way traits can be categorized is by whether they are *dominant* or *recessive*. Dominant traits have a higher probability of expressing themselves than recessive ones.

There's an easy way to observe recessive traits in people around you.

MATERIALS NEEDED:
- Notebook to record observations
- Pen

PROCEDURE:
1. Have your child look at all of his family members' eyes and record the colors of each person's eyes. Have him divide eye color into two categories: brown and blue (green eyes can be placed in the same category as blue for simplicity).
2. If your own family members all have the same color eyes (all brown or all blue), then tell your child to look for a family

that has mixed color eyes (perhaps the family of a school friend). Have him check the eye color of each member of that family and record his observations in his notebook.

3. Have your child record his observations for some other families that are known to him.

Now it's time for your child to examine his observations. Did he find one family where one parent had brown eyes while the other had blue eyes, yet all the children had brown eyes? If so, then he found the mostly dominant trait for eye color. Brown is the mostly dominant color of eyes. If one parent has entirely brown-eye genes, then most likely all the children of that parent will have brown eyes.

STEM Q&A

Who is the father of genetics?

Gregor Johann Mendel lived in the nineteenth century, and is known as the father of genetics. He was from a region known today as the Czech Republic. His experiments on pea plants enabled him to understand how certain traits were inherited, establishing the rules of heredity. He coined the terms "dominant" and "recessive" to describe certain traits.

If the parent with brown eyes carried the genes for blue eyes, the blue-eye trait would not necessarily show up in that parent. But if that parent mates with another parent who has blue eyes, then the blue-eye genes have a higher chance of showing up in the children. When blue-eye genes from both parents show up together, then the child can have blue eyes. In other words, the parent with brown eyes can possibly carry the genes that can participate in the making of blue eyes in the children.

If the entire family has blue eyes in several generations, most likely all members of the family have only blue-eye genes. It would be very rare for anyone in that family to have brown eyes.

Geneticist

Geneticists study genes. Genetics deals with traits that get passed down from one generation to the next. They may help shed light on a person's health based on family history in terms of hereditary diseases.

Many jobs for a geneticist are in the medical fields and clinical research. Geneticists perform tests and interpret their results, often to individuals and their family members for whom the tests were made. Geneticists may work in other sectors such as law and public policy, as well as education. They may also work in the private sector with biotechnology companies.

CHAPTER 7

MATHEMATICS AND COMPUTER SCIENCE

Some of the coolest, most interesting jobs being created in today's economy are in fields related to mathematics and computer science. You might have a hard time convincing some people of that fact, but it certainly is true. Professionals with math and computer training are changing the way business is done and life is lived. They're working with data, gleaning all the intelligence they can from figures in spreadsheets and data files. Some of them are creating secret codes and encrypting data, while others (such as military and security experts) are busy honing their code-breaking skills. Some math and computer science professionals help create and oversee the systems that power the economy, moving dollars and other currencies around the globe, and calculating the probabilities of various events occurring. In addition to being among the most intellectually stimulating of all career fields, jobs involving mathematics and science tend to be among the highest paid. If the activities in this chapter stimulate your child's interest, he or she might be naturally cut out for a career related to math or computer science.

DESIGNING WALLPAPER USING PERCENTAGES

This simple activity is fun for artistic kids, especially those with a flair for design. It also offers them an easy way to visualize percentages.

MATERIALS NEEDED:
- 100-square grid
- A set of fine-tip colored markers

You can design your own 100-square grid on blank paper using a straight edge, or you can find a grid online to print out. Just do a search for "Blank 100 Grid." If you download a grid from an online source, be sure it actually has 100 blank squares (count 10 columns across the top and 10 rows across the side).

The Setup

For this activity, tell your child that her task is to create a design for some new wallpaper on the 100-square grid. She can use some artistic license in the design, but there are some requirements for the new wallpaper:

WALLPAPER DESIGN SPECS:
- 30 percent of the squares must contain stars
- 20 percent of the squares must contain half-moons
- 25 percent of the squares must be shaded blue
- 15 percent of the squares must be shaded gray, silver, or purple
- 10 percent of the squares must be kept blank

Percentage Basics

After your child has completed her design, use it as a basis for discussing percentages. *Percent* simply means per hundred. Fifty percent, or half, of the squares in the wallpaper design have shapes inside them (i.e., stars or moons). Twenty-five percent (or a quarter) of the squares are shaded blue.

Decimals can easily be converted into percentages. Simply multiply the decimal number by 100 and place the % symbol after the resulting number. For example, 0.25 can be converted into a percentage by multiplying it by 100 and placing % after the number. So 0.25 × 100 = 25%.

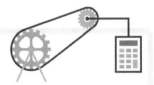

STEM Q&A

Does it matter whether you use decimals or percentages?

Decimals and percentages both represent parts of a whole. Technically speaking, since one can easily be converted into the other, it doesn't matter whether you use decimals or percentages. However, decimals make more sense in certain contexts, and percentages make more sense in others. For instance, survey results are usually given in percentage terms (e.g., 62% of American households include at least one pet). Decimals are more often used in measurements, especially when accuracy is important (e.g., measurements in a scientific lab).

To convert a percentage into a decimal number you simply reverse the procedure. Remove the % symbol and divide the number by 100. For instance, suppose you want to convert 49% into a decimal. After removing the percent sign, you simply divide 49 by 100. So 49% is equivalent to 0.49. Since fractions also represent parts of a whole, they can be converted into percentages. The easiest way to convert a fraction into a percentage is to first convert the fraction into a decimal number by dividing the fraction's numerator by its denominator. After that's done, multiply the resulting decimal number by 100 and place the % sign after it.

Mathematician

Some would argue that mathematics is one of the oldest sciences known to man. Most people who work in most STEM fields need some math knowledge. Mathematicians are the real diehards, the ones who eat and breathe proofs and algorithms. Some mathematicians work in theoretical mathematics, meaning that they work to discover new math principles. Because most theoretical mathematicians work at universities as professors, they must earn doctorate degrees in mathematics to enter the field. Other mathematicians work in applied mathematics, meaning that they look for ways to use math principles to solve real-world problems. Universities hire applied mathematicians, and so do government agencies and some private companies. Many applied mathematicians also earn doctorate degrees, but there are jobs available in the field for master's degree holders. A math major will increase her marketability by also taking some classes in statistics and computer science.

ACTIVITY:

TIC-TAC-TOE MATH REVIEW

Tic-tac-toe is one of the fastest and easiest games to play. It's also an easy game to adapt into a math review activity. It can be used for any level of math and for any math concept. Of course, with the math review component, the game will take longer to complete.

MATERIALS NEEDED:

- Paper
- Pen or pencil
- A supply of math review questions

Game play for the Tic-Tac-Toe Math Review is similar to the way the game is typically played. The difference is that after drawing a three-by-three grid on your paper, you populate the nine squares with math review problems. For longer, more complex problems, you'll of course need a larger grid with larger squares.

Computer Programmer

If it weren't for computer programmers, we wouldn't enjoy all the technological tools and toys we do today. We wouldn't have cell phone apps—or even smartphones! Computer programmers are responsible for all those cool apps and games. They also write programs that help businesses and other organizations function more smoothly. Computer programmers write and test code—not secret spy code, but code that tells computers what to do (and when to do it). Most computer programmers have bachelor's degrees in computer science, but some find work with an associate's degree. Most individuals in the field specialize in a few programming languages, such as SQL, Java, C++, Python, etc.

When it's a player's turn, he doesn't just choose a box and fill it with an X or O, as with standard play. First he must successfully complete the math review problem in the box he wishes to claim. If the player finds the correct solution to the problem, he fills in his X or O. If he doesn't answer correctly, he can attempt another review question in a different box. On his next turn, he may reattempt the problem previously missed, if the other player hasn't already claimed that box.

Following are six sets of problems you can use to populate the squares in your tic-tac-toe game. The problems cover six different topic areas (for convenience, answers are provided in parentheses).

MULTIPLICATION:

- 10×9 (90)
- 7×11 (77)
- 5×15 (75)
- 6×12 (72)
- 8×14 (112)

- 7×30 (210)
- 3×22 (66)
- 2×18 (36)
- 10×20 (200)

DIVISION:

- $100 \div 10$ (10)
- $88 \div 11$ (8)
- $72 \div 9$ (8)
- $120 \div 40$ (3)
- $144 \div 12$ (12)

- $250 \div 5$ (50)
- $90 \div 15$ (6)
- $99 \div 33$ (3)
- $1,000 \div 200$ (5)

SIMPLIFYING FRACTIONS:

- $\frac{5}{10}$ ($\frac{1}{2}$)
- $\frac{4}{12}$ ($\frac{1}{3}$)
- $\frac{2}{8}$ ($\frac{1}{4}$)
- $\frac{10}{25}$ ($\frac{2}{5}$)
- $\frac{9}{81}$ ($\frac{1}{9}$)

- $\frac{20}{30}$ ($\frac{2}{3}$)
- $\frac{7}{7}$ (1)
- $\frac{6}{8}$ ($\frac{3}{4}$)
- $\frac{100}{1000}$ ($\frac{1}{10}$)

ADDING AND SUBTRACTING DECIMALS:

- 0.10 + 0.35 (0.45)
- 0.02 + 0.03 (0.05)
- 0.50–0.20 (0.30)
- 0.33–0.03 (0.30)
- 0.65–0.15 (0.50)

- 0.12 + 0.08 (0.20)
- 0.80 + 0.20 (1.00)
- 0.01 + 0.14 (0.15)
- 0.95–0.35 (0.60)

EXPONENTS:

- 2^3 (8)
- 4^2 (16)
- 5^4 (625)
- 10^2 (100)
- 11^2 (121)

- 3^3 (27)
- 4^4 (256)
- 2^5 (32)
- 2^8 (256)

SOLVING FOR AN UNKNOWN:

- 4 + X = 6 (2)
- 7 + X = 10 (3)
- 12–X = 6 (6)
- 2X = 8 (4)
- 3 / X = 3 (1)

- X–2 = 9 (11)
- X / 2 = 4 (8)
- 5X = 15 (3)
- X + 9 = 17 (8)

STEM Words to Know

exponent

An exponent is shorthand notation for raising a number to a particular power. For example, 4^3 is 4 raised to the 3rd power, which is like writing 4 × 4 × 4. Note that in that example, the number 4 is known as the *base* and 3 is the *exponent* or the *power*.

For some of the topics you'll want to keep plenty of scratch paper on hand. Also encourage your child to create his own math review questions for use in the tic-tac-toe game. Encourage him to create some basic questions and some more challenging ones that he can't easily answer in his head.

Does the Order of Operations Really Matter?

Order of operations can matter a lot if you're solving a problem involving more than one mathematical operation. Consider the problem 5–4 ÷ 2. Without a predetermined order of operations, you could solve the problem by subtracting 4 from 5 and dividing the result by 2, giving you an answer of ½. Alternatively you could solve the problem by dividing 2 into 4 and subtracting the result from 5, which gives you an answer of 3. Both ½ and 3 can't be correct. The rules of math say you should first perform any operations that are inside parentheses. Then you should take care of any exponents or roots. After that, perform any multiplication and division, working from left to right. Lastly, take care of all addition and subtraction, again moving from left to right. Based on the standard order of operations, 3 is the correct answer to the problem.

Computer Systems Analyst

The work computer systems analysts do is different from what computer programmers do. Computer systems analysts focus on improving an organization's computer systems and procedures so that they operate as efficiently as possible. Because of the nature of their work, computer systems analysts must be good problem solvers. Most systems analysts have at least a bachelor's degree in computer or information science, but some organizations hire grads from other degree areas who also possess IT (information technology) skills. Over the next decade, the demand for computer systems analysts is expected to grow much faster than the average demand for all occupations in the United States.

ACTIVITY:
ALGEBRA DICE

Use this simple dice game to introduce your child to basic algebra. *Algebra* is a branch of mathematics in which symbols are used to represent numbers in equations or formulas. Typically, the symbols are letters of the alphabet, such as X or Y. Your child may get so caught up in the game that she may not even realize she's doing algebra.

MATERIALS NEEDED:
- Pair of standard dice
- Blank sheet of paper
- Pen or marker
- Scratch paper and a pencil
- Watch or timer (optional)

Game Setup

You'll first design a game board using the blank sheet of paper and the marker or pen. There are several variations of the game you can play. Choose whichever best suits your child's current math abilities—though don't be afraid to challenge her to think a little beyond them.

In the simplest version of the game, you'll set up the board for addition problems. Using a marker or pen, write ___ + X = ___ on the blank sheet of paper. The spaces should each be about 1½"–2" in width.

Game Play

Algebra Dice is super simple to play. Have your child roll the pair of dice. Place the die with the larger value over the blank on the right side, after the equals sign. Place the other die, the one with the smaller value, over the blank on the left. Explain to your child that the X represents an unknown in the equation. Her task is to figure out what number can be put in place of X to make the equation true. Each time you roll the dice, you create a new equation with a new X to solve. The goal of the game is to solve as many Xs as possible in ten minutes. It may be easier for your child to visualize the problem if, after rolling the dice each time, she rewrites the equation on scratch paper using standard numerals in place of the dots on the dice.

A Strategy for Playing the Game

If your child hasn't yet worked with equations in math class, she can still play the game. You'll just need to provide her with a strategy for solving the unknown X.

Data Architect

There are numerous specialized job functions and titles within the information technology world. Some titles include data architect, cloud architect, and systems engineer, among others. The distinction among these various roles becomes more critical later on in a person's job selection process. Many of these positions require similar training at the undergraduate level. To give an example of the differences in the roles, consider a data architect versus a database administrator. Just as an architect creates the designs that are used to construct a house, a data architect designs the structure that will house an organization's data. In contrast, a database administrator maintains the organization's database on a day-to-day basis (e.g., backing up data and keeping it secure). Data and databases are so important to companies and other organizations that, since the dawn of the information age, several other related occupations have cropped up, including data modeler, data analyst, and data scientist. All would be excellent for a person with IT skills who also happens to be a good problem solver.

Explain to her that the equation on the game board is like a scale—not a bathroom scale with a digital readout, but an old-time scale like the proverbial scales of justice (show her a picture from the Internet if necessary). Like those old scales, an equation has to balance out. If one side of the equation has a larger total value than the other side, the equation is out of balance.

For example, if you roll a 6 and a 2 on the dice, the equation on the game board will read $2 + X = 6$. What number could be put in place of X to make this equation balance out?

The standard way of approaching this type of problem in math is to isolate the unknown X. Since the two sides of the equation need to balance out, whatever operation is done on the left side of the equation must also be done on the right side. To isolate the X in this example, you would need to subtract 2 from the left side of the equation; then the only value remaining on the left side would be X. But when you subtract 2 from the left side, you also need to subtract 2 from the right side: 2 subtracted from 6 leaves a difference of 4. So after subtracting 2 from each side of the equation, what remains is $X = 4$. And that is the solution for the unknown X. Following this strategy, the unknown becomes known.

Variations of the Game

One way to make Algebra Dice a bit more challenging is to allow for negative values of the unknown X. Instead of rolling the dice at the same time and placing the larger value on the right, roll each die individually and the place the first die rolled on the right and the second one rolled on the left. You will inevitably have outcomes such as $5 + X = 3$. This problem can be solved following the same strategy as outlined previously; the value of the X just turns out to be a negative number.

Another way to raise the level of challenge is to create new game boards featuring different math operations. Following are some suggested ways of setting up the game board:

$$\_\_\_ - X = \_\_\_$$
$$X - \_\_\_ = \_\_\_$$
$$\_\_\_ X = \_\_\_ \text{ or } (\_\_\_)(X) = \_\_\_$$
$$\_\_\_ / X = \_\_\_$$
$$X / \_\_\_ = \_\_\_$$

Each time you introduce a new operation, you may need to walk your child through the strategy for solving for X. The same basic principle applies: The two sides of the equation should remain in balance, so whatever operation is done on the right side must be done on the left.

For example, suppose the equation that comes up in the game is $3X = 6$. The X can be isolated by dividing the left side of the equation by 3: 3X divided by 3 leaves X. The right side of the equation must also be divided by 3: 6 divided by 3 is 2, so in this case $X = 2$.

CALCULATING THE CIRCUMFERENCE OF A PIE, BIKE WHEEL, CAR TIRE, ETC.

How many circular objects can you find around the house? Ask your child to find some circles, and then practice finding the circumference of those objects.

MATERIALS NEEDED:
- Tape measure
- Various circular objects
- Calculator

Circle Basics

Even a very young child can identify a circle, but not everyone knows what *makes* a circle a circle, technically speaking. A circle is a plane shape whose outer points are all the same distance from its center. The distance around the edge of a circle is the *circumference*. A line through the center, or midpoint, of a circle that connects two of the circle's outer points is called the *diameter*. If you cut a pie precisely in half, right down the middle, you're tracing the pie's diameter. Half of a circle's diameter is its *radius*. A radius connects a circle's center or midpoint with a point on the circle's border.

STEM Words to Know

chord

A chord is a straight line connecting two points on a circle's border. The diameter of a circle is a chord, but of course not all chords are the diameter. A circle's radius is not a chord, because a radius only touches one point on the circle's border.

Calculating the Circumference

The formula for calculating a circle's circumference is relatively easy to use. The circumference can be found by multiplying the circle's diameter by the numerical constant known as *pi*, denoted by the Greek symbol π. The number *pi* is represented by the sixteenth letter in the Greek alphabet, π. It is the ratio of a circle's circumference to its diameter, π = circumference/diameter. The value of π is approximately 3.14159 , but the digits go on infinitely without repeating. The formula is written as:

$$C = \pi \cdot d$$

C represents the circle's circumference and *d* represents the diameter. Because a circle's radius is half its diameter, the circumference can also be found using the formula:

$$C = 2\pi \cdot r$$

where *r* stands for radius.

The Circle Challenge

Help your child master the circumference formula by challenging her to find several circular objects around the house and measuring the circumference of those items. If more than one child is involved, set it up as a little contest to see who can find the biggest circle, who can find the smallest circle, and who can find the most circles. If your child has trouble locating circles, you can steer her toward a few to get her started. Here are a few ideas:

- Bike tire
- Car tire
- Plate
- Ring
- Compact case
- Butter tub lid
- Round tabletop
- Bottom of a mug
- Circular pattern on a rug or throw

- Drumhead
- Actual pie (frozen or baked)

Encourage your child to try out both versions of the circumference formula, perhaps even on the same object. Have her choose a circle, measure its diameter, and then, using a calculator, multiply the circle's diameter by 3.14159. Or, alternatively, she can measure the radius, multiply it by 2, and multiply that product by pi. This activity will help your child learn to use a tape measure while reinforcing the basic geometry of circles.

Calculating the Area of a Circle

Consider taking the activity a step further and ask your child to calculate the area of some of the circles she found. The area of a circle is calculated using

$$A = \pi \cdot r^2$$

where A represents the circle's area and r represents the circle's radius. Note that π also shows up in the formula for the area of a circle. Not only is π a famous number, it's also very useful in geometry.

Database Administrator

As the job title implies, database administrators are responsible for maintaining the databases of the organizations they work for. They're responsible for backing up data and keeping the databases secure. Most people with this job have a bachelor's degree in computer science or some related field. Because data is an integral part of companies' everyday business activities, the role of database administrators will continue to grow in importance in the future. According to the Bureau of Labor Statistics, the demand for database administrators will grow faster than the average demand for all U.S. occupations in the coming years.

THE CARTESIAN TREASURE MAP

The Cartesian Treasure Map is a fun activity that can be used to reinforce a child's understanding of the coordinate system. It's essentially a board game you can make yourself.

MATERIALS NEEDED:
- Graph paper
- Felt-tip pen
- Ruler or other straight edge
- Crayons or markers

Begin with a clean sheet of graph paper (a number of websites offer downloadable graph paper free of charge). Using a straight edge and a felt-tip pen, draw two lines, dividing the page into four parts or four quadrants. If you want to be exact, you can take measurements to ensure that your lines are precisely centered. These two lines form the axes for your coordinates. Decide which axis will be your x (or horizontal) axis, and which will be your y (or vertical) axis. After you've decided, orient your page appropriately.

STEM Words to Know

Cartesian plane

The Cartesian plane, also known as the x-y plane, is divided into four quadrants numbered I through IV. In Quadrant I, the upper right-hand quadrant, both the x and y coordinates are positive. In Quadrant II, the upper left-hand quadrant, the x value is negative and the y value is positive. In Quadrant III, the lower left-hand quadrant, both the coordinates are negative. In Quadrant IV, the lower right-hand quadrant, the x value is positive and the y value is negative.

Number the x and y axes. The point where the two lines intersect is the *origin*, whose coordinates are 0 on the x axis and 0 and the y axis. (It's not necessary to label the origin.) From the origin, begin numbering the points to the right along the horizontal axis. As you move the pen rightward from the origin, the numbers increase (i.e., the point on the x axis one place to the right of the origin is 1, the point two places to the right of the origin is 2, and so on). As you move the pen leftward from the origin, the numbers decrease (i.e., the point on the x axis one place to the left of the origin is –1, the point two places to the left of the origin is –2, and so on).

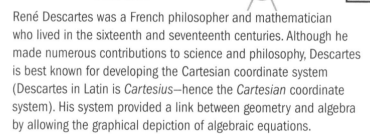

STEM Q&A

Who was Descartes?

René Descartes was a French philosopher and mathematician who lived in the sixteenth and seventeenth centuries. Although he made numerous contributions to science and philosophy, Descartes is best known for developing the Cartesian coordinate system (Descartes in Latin is *Cartesius*—hence the *Cartesian* coordinate system). His system provided a link between geometry and algebra by allowing the graphical depiction of algebraic equations.

As you set out to number the y or vertical axis, keep in mind that the numbers increase moving up the axis and decrease moving down the axis. The point on the y axis one place above the origin is 1, the point two places above the origin is 2, and so on. The point on the y axis one place below the origin is –1, the point two places below the origin is –2, and so on.

After you've numbered your axes, your coordinate system is ready. You could use it just as it is for a learning activity, but your child will probably have more fun if you dress it up a bit. Invite your child to use crayons or markers to transform the page into a pirate treasure map. Keep in mind that pirate treasure maps are typically quite different from the ordinary kind of map you'd find in an automobile glove box. Common features on a pirate treasure map include islands, palm trees, ships, volcanoes, caves, and skulls. Make sure the number lines remain visible as your child decorates the treasure map.

Using the Map

Of course, everyone knows that an X on a pirate map marks the spot where treasure is buried. You could stick with one X per map, but there's nothing that says you can't have more than one treasure marked on your map. Mark some Xs on the map, preferably at least one in each quadrant and one on the origin.

Geospatial Analyst

Geospatial analysts work with geographic data in what are known as *geographic information systems (GIS)*. Some geospatial analysts are involved in *geocoding*, which is the process of adding geographic data to a database. Such map-based data typically include features about a particular location, such as terrain, roads, population, income level, etc. Geographic information systems are used for many purposes, including transportation and utility planning (e.g., placement of gas and electric lines), market research, and environmental studies.

Create a little story for use with the activity. Have your child pretend that he's the pirate captain and he has to direct his crew to the spots on the map where the treasures are located. How will he direct them to the proper locations? Of course he'll use Cartesian x-y coordinates!

The x-y coordinates are always given in a particular order. The x value is always given first, and the y value second. Together, a pair of x-y coordinates (known as an *ordered pair*) designates a particular point on a graph—or, in the case of this activity, a particular point on the map. The x value in the ordered pair gives the horizontal distance from the origin, and the y value gives the vertical distance from the origin.

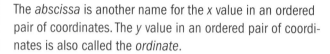

STEM Words to Know

abscissa

The *abscissa* is another name for the x value in an ordered pair of coordinates. The y value in an ordered pair of coordinates is also called the *ordinate*.

For example, the pair of coordinates (3, 2) refers to the point that is three places to the right of the origin on the x axis and two places up on the y axis. The pair of coordinates (–5, –10) refers to the point that's five places to the left of the origin on the x axis and ten places down on the y axis. The pair (6, –4) refers to the point that's six places to the right of the origin on the x axis and four places down on the y axis. The origin has the coordinates (0, 0).

After your child successfully "locates" all the treasures by assigning them pairs of coordinates, consider rewarding him with a real treasure. Treats work as well as gold doubloons for hungry pirate captains! You might also consider trying other activities that use the Cartesian plane. For example, work with your child to create a map of your neighborhood, and then ask him to identify coordinates for particular points in the neighborhood.

THE GEOMETRY SCAVENGER HUNT

Students tend to become more interested in a subject when they can see its relevance to their daily lives. The Geometry Scavenger Hunt is a simple activity you can use to help your child learn to identify geometric shapes while gaining an appreciation for the importance of geometry in everyday life.

MATERIALS NEEDED:
- List of geometric shapes (see following)
- Pencil or pen

One person can do the Geometry Scavenger Hunt alone, or it can be set up as a challenge involving two or more scavenger hunters. If your child is hunting alone, challenge her to find as many shapes on the list as she can. To increase the intensity level of the hunt you can consider adding a time limit. If more than one hunter is involved, conduct the activity like a standard scavenger hunt—i.e., the hunter who finds the most shapes by the end of the game wins.

STEM Q&A

Who was Euclid?

Euclid was a Greek mathematician who lived around 300 B.C. and taught mathematics in Alexandria, Egypt. Often referred to as the "Father of Geometry," Euclid wrote the most important work in the field of geometry, *Elements*. One of the most studied texts in human history, Euclid's *Elements* carefully presents the axioms, theorems, constructions, and proofs that have come to be known collectively as Euclidean geometry.

GEOMETRY SCAVENGER HUNT—LIST OF SHAPES:

- ❏ Right angle—an angle measuring 90 degrees
- ❏ Acute angle—an angle measuring between 0 and 90 degrees
- ❏ Obtuse angle—an angle measuring between 90 and 180 degrees
- ❏ Circle—a plane shape with all of its outer points the same distance from its center
- ❏ Polygon—a plane shape with straight sides
- ❏ Quadrilateral—a 4-sided polygon with 4 angles
- ❏ Parallelogram—a quadrilateral with 2 pairs of parallel sides
- ❏ Rhombus—a parallelogram with 4 equal sides
- ❏ Rectangle—a parallelogram with 4 sides and 4 right angles
- ❏ Square—a rectangle with 4 equal sides
- ❏ Pentagon—a 5-sided polygon
- ❏ Octagon—an 8-sided polygon
- ❏ Equilateral triangle—a triangle with three equal sides and three equal angles
- ❏ Isosceles triangle—a triangle with two equal sides and two equal interior angles
- ❏ Scalene triangle—a triangle with no equal sides and no equal angles
- ❏ Acute triangle—a triangle whose interior angles are all less than 90 degrees
- ❏ Right triangle—a triangle with one 90-degree interior angle
- ❏ Obtuse triangle—a triangle with an interior angle that's greater than 90 degrees
- ❏ Cube—a three-dimensional solid object with 6 identical square faces
- ❏ Sphere—a three-dimensional (ball-shaped) object whose surface points are all equidistant from the center
- ❏ Cylinder—a three-dimensional solid object with two parallel circular or elliptical ends and a curved outer surface
- ❏ Cone—a three-dimensional solid object with a flat circular base that tapers to a single point

Be creative in hunting for shapes. The screen on a flat-screen TV is a rectangle. A drink coaster may be circular. A pattern on a rug might include many shapes in the list.

The Geometry Scavenger Hunt for Younger Children

If you have younger children, try a scaled-down version of the Geometry Scavenger Hunt, using the following list.

GEOMETRY SCAVENGER HUNT— LIST OF SHAPES (SHORT VERSION):

- ❏ Line
- ❏ Circle
- ❏ Square
- ❏ Rectangle
- ❏ Triangle
- ❏ Star
- ❏ Cube
- ❏ Sphere
- ❏ Cone

Either version of the scavenger hunt can be done at home or at any location where shapes abound. Consider trying it with your children as a driving game the next time you set out on a family road trip.

MEAN, MEDIAN, AND MODE

Statisticians are people who work with numbers every day. Statisticians analyze a group of numbers, which is often referred to as a *data set*, or just data. The numbers in a data set represent counts or measurements from real life. For example, if you look up the win-loss record of your favorite sports team, you're looking at data. If you count the number of students in your classroom who are wearing short sleeves versus the number who are wearing long sleeves, you're working with data.

When statisticians work with a set of data, there are certain things they typically want to know about it. For instance, they often want to know where the center of a set of data lies. There are three common methods statisticians use to find the center (i.e., point of central tendency) of a data set. Each method has a different name, and the answers they yield aren't always the same.

Mean

You've probably come across *mean* before, but it you may have heard it called a different name. Mean is the same as average. Suppose the heights of the five starting players on the Rockaway Blasters basketball team are as follows:

Joe	10 ft. (yes, that's really, really tall!)
Jenny	6 ft.
Jordan	5 ft.
Jehan	5 ft.
J.J.	4 ft.

The collection of the players' heights is a data set with 5 values. You might be able to make a guess about the central point of this data set by just eyeballing it, but there's no need to guess. The mean, or average, can easily be calculated by summing the 5 values and dividing that sum by the total number of values in the data set.

$$10 + 6 + 5 + 5 + 4 = 30$$
$$30 / 5 = 6$$

The mean height of a starting player on the Rockaway Blasters basketball team is 6 feet.

STEM Words to Know

arithmetic mean

The mean, or what people often call the average, is technically known as the *arithmetic mean*. There are actually other means used in mathematics, such as the weighted mean and the geometric mean, but the arithmetic mean is by far the most commonly used mean concept.

Median

After calculating the mean for the data set, you might think your work is done. But if you examine the values in the data set more closely and compare them to the mean, you may realize that 6 feet is not very representative of the typical Rockaway starting player's height. In fact, three of the players are significantly less than 6 feet tall.

You've calculated the mean correctly. The problem lies in the fact that one of the players, Joe, is a *lot* taller than all the other players. Joe's height skews the data set such that the mean is not very representative of the typical player's height. Joe is what statisticians refer to as an *outlier*, meaning that his height doesn't fit neatly with the rest of the data.

When a data set has outliers like Joe, the *median* is usually a better indicator of the data set's center. The median is the value that falls exactly at the halfway point in a data set. For example, in a data set composed of the values 1, 2, and 3, the point in the middle, or the median, is 2.

The easiest way to find the median is to first arrange the values in a given data set from smallest to largest. Suppose a data set contains the following values: 100, 35, 15, 20, 5.

Arranged from smallest to largest they are:

5, 15, 20, 35, 100

After the values are arranged from smallest to largest, the next step is to cross out the smallest value and the largest value in the set. Neither value is the median.

5, 15, 20, 35, ~~100~~

STEM Words to Know

range

Another measure that is sometimes useful when working with data is the *range*. It's easy to calculate the range of a set of numbers. Simply subtract the smallest value in the data set from the largest value in the data set. The resulting answer is the range. For example, if the largest value is 100 and the smallest value is 5, the range is 100 – 5 = 95. The range gives you an idea of the scope of the data you're working with.

Cross out the next smallest value and the next largest value in the set. Those aren't the median, either.

5, ~~15~~, 20, ~~35~~, ~~100~~

This process of elimination is continued until there's only one remaining value—the one exactly in the middle. That value is the median. In this last example, the median is 20. But what if a data set contains an even number of values? Consider a data set made up of the following values:

60, 70, 80, 90

When the smallest and largest values are crossed out, there are two values remaining.

~~60~~, 70, 80, ~~90~~

In a situation where there are two middle values, the median is determined by finding the mean of those two middle values.

70 + 80 = 150
150 / 2 = 75

The data set 60, 70, 80, 90 has a median of 75.

Back to the Rockaway Blasters basketball team and their starting lineup. Again, the heights of the starting players are 10 feet, 6 feet, 5 feet, 5 feet, and 4 feet.

Arranged from smallest to largest, the players' heights are:

4, 5, 5, 6, 10

Following the procedure already outlined, it should be clear that the median height of the starting players is 5 feet.

4, 5, 5, 6, 10

In the case of the Rockaway Blasters starting lineup, because Joe's height is so much different from the other players, the median is a better indicator of the data set's central point than the mean.

Mode

In some situations, the best representation of a typical value in a data set is given by the *mode*. The mode is simply the value in the data set that repeats most frequently. In the data set containing the heights of the Rockaway Blasters starting basketball team—4, 5, 5, 6, 10—the value 5 occurs twice (i.e., there are two players who are 5 feet tall). The mode of the data set is 5, or 5 feet.

STEM Q&A

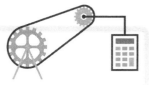

Is the mode always a good measure of central tendency?

One shortcoming of the mode as a measure of central tendency is the fact that not every data set has a mode. What if the players' heights were 4 feet, 5 feet, 6 feet, 7 feet, and 10 feet? None of the values repeat, so there's no mode. It's also the case that some data sets have more than one mode. What if the heights of the Rockaway starters were 5 feet, 5 feet, 6 feet, 6 feet, and 10 feet? The value 5 feet occurs twice in the data set and so does the value 6 feet. This data set has *two* modes.

Some Practice with Mean, Median, and Mode

The next time you're at a gathering of family or friends, have your child ask everyone in attendance their age. Then the two of you can calculate the mean age of those in attendance. Also calculate the median and mode. See if you can identify any obvious outliers (i.e., friends or family members who are significantly younger or older than the others in attendance).

Have your child ask all of her classmates how many TVs are in their home. Find the mean, median, and mode number of TVs.

Keep track of how much money you spend each day for a month. At the end of the month, calculate the mean amount you spent per day. Also calculate the median and mode. The results may surprise you.

Statistician

Statisticians collect, process, and analyze data using various statistical techniques. Some statisticians use data to make predictions about the future. Nearly all statisticians utilize computer programs to help them complete their analyses. Lots of companies in a wide array of industries hire statisticians. These days it would be hard to find an industry in which statistics is not applied in some manner. Government agencies also use statisticians to prepare and analyze government data. A degree in mathematics doesn't necessarily qualify a person for a career as a statistician. Statisticians need specialized training in statistical principles and methods, along with training in one or more of the prominent statistical analysis software packages. A graduate degree in statistics is, of course, the best training for a person who wishes to pursue a career as a statistician. A bachelor's degree may be enough to land someone an entry-level job in the field.

PIES AND BARS

Organizing and presenting data is an important part of statistics. There are several ways data can be displayed visually. Data can be presented in a table, a graph, or a chart. One of the most common graphic forms for data display is the tried-and-true pie chart.

Pie Chart Basics

Everyone who's flipped through magazines or newspapers has seen pie charts. Popular periodicals such as *USA Today* frequently use pie charts to present data in an easily digestible manner.

Here's an example of a pie chart that shows the causes of airline delay.

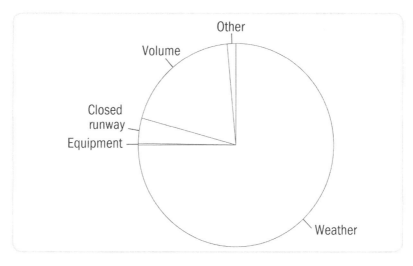

The whole circle or "pie" represents the full universe of reasons why flights might be delayed. Each section, or piece of the pie, represents a particular reason why flights may be delayed. As you might gather from examining the pie chart, the biggest reason for flight delays is weather. The least significant reason for flight delays is equipment failure. The sizes of the sections of the pie chart correspond to the data represented in the chart. Pie charts are easy to interpret when they're used properly.

Making a Pie Chart by Hand

There are a number of computer programs you can use to generate accurate pie charts. However, if your child goes through the process of creating one by hand, he'll have a better understanding of the mechanics of pie charts and of how the underlying data fits into the chart. He'll also get a little practice with some basic geometry concepts.

MATERIALS NEEDED:
- Blank paper
- Pencil
- Compass
- Protractor
- Set of colored pencils or markers

You'll want to begin by converting your "raw" data into percentages. An example will help clarify the process. Suppose you have ten people living in your household, and you have your child go around and ask each one his or her favorite flavor of ice cream. Suppose your child discovers from his survey that 5 of the people in your household like chocolate ice cream the best, 3 like vanilla the best, and 2 prefer strawberry. In percentage terms, $5/10$ or 50% of the members of your household prefer chocolate, 30% prefer vanilla, and 20% like strawberry the best.

After your child has converted his raw data into percentages, have him pause for a moment to add up the resulting percentages. If they don't total 100%, he needs to check over his work; the percentages should add up to 100.

The next step involves a little geometry. Keeping in mind that a whole circle is 360 degrees, he'll want to multiply each of his percentages from the first step by 360. This will give him the angles he needs to create each section of the pie chart.

50% × 360 degrees = 180 degrees
30% × 360 degrees = 108 degrees
20% × 360 degrees = 72 degrees

At this point he may want to pause and check his math again. Be sure the degrees add up to 360. If the math checks out, then he's ready to begin drawing his pie chart.

STEM Words to Know

raw data

Raw data is data that hasn't yet been processed—much like raw food is food that hasn't yet been processed. If you ask three different people their ages and write down their responses, you've gathered raw data. If you calculate the average, or mean, of those three ages, then the data has been processed; it's no longer raw data.

He should start by drawing a circle on a blank piece of paper using the compass. Make the circle large so that he can easily divide it into slices. There should be an indentation in the paper, in the circle's center, where the compass needle rested. From that center, he can draw a straight line to the edge of the circle. Then, using the protractor, he should measure out his first angle and draw the corresponding line on the chart. Returning to the ice cream flavor example, the first angle is 180 degrees. After measuring a 180-degree angle and drawing the line, he will have cut the pie exactly in half.

Next he'll measure out the remaining angles and draw the corresponding lines, sectioning the circle into the appropriately sized slices. In the ice cream example, there will obviously be three sections or slices.

The sections of a pie chart are typically color-coded to a key. After your child has converted the raw data into percentages and calculated and drawn the angles, he can choose a color to represent each section of the pie and shade in the sections. Lastly, he can create a color key along one side of the page explaining the meaning of each color in the pie chart.

An Additional Pie Chart Activity

After your child successfully creates the pie chart in the example, invite him to try another one from scratch. The extra step of gathering the raw data will help him see the connection between real-world information and two-dimensional charts and graphs.

The same materials are required as those listed in the previous activity. The only difference is that your child will gather his own data. Have him ask ten friends or classmates one of the following questions and carefully record the answers:

- What's your favorite sport to watch on TV?
- What's your favorite subject in school?
- What's your favorite holiday?
- What's your favorite season?

STEM Words to Know

mutually exclusive

When categories are mutually exclusive it means that items can only belong to one category at a time. For example, "dead" and "alive" are generally considered to be mutually exclusive categories. A person or an animal can't be both dead and alive at the same time. The seasons of the year are also mutually exclusive categories. You can't find a date on the calendar that falls both in the spring and the summer because the seasons have clearly defined beginnings and endings.

When he's gathering the data, it's important that each person surveyed give only one response. It doesn't work if someone says he likes Thanksgiving and Halloween equally, unless your child collects responses such as those into a category called "Undecided" or something similar. For the pie chart to make sense, the categories represented by the sections must be *mutually exclusive*.

After your child gathers the data, guide him through the steps outlined previously. It might be interesting to try creating the pie chart using Excel or another chart generator, and then compare the computer version to the home-grown one.

Market Research Analyst

Businesses are always trying to figure out what customers want. Market research analysts study market conditions and trends to determine whether or not products are meeting consumers' needs, how products can be improved, and the best ways companies can communicate information about their products to potential consumers. Market research analysts gather data and attempt to spot trends in the data. Sometimes they identify new markets for old products. They also help companies figure out which of their advertising and marketing methods are bringing in the most customers. Market research analysts must have strong analytical skills, so classes in statistics, mathematics, and economics will prove useful, alongside their marketing classes. Most market research analysts will also need to learn the ins and outs of one or more of the prominent software packages used in the field.

Bar Chart Basics

The *bar chart* is another widely used graphical display for certain types of data. A bar chart—also called a *bar graph*—uses bars to represent data in various categories. The bars' heights (or lengths) are proportional to the data being presented. The bars on a bar chart can be vertical or horizontal. Note that in Excel a bar chart uses horizontal bars. In Excel, a chart that uses vertical bars is called a *column chart*.

Suppose you and your child want to create a bar chart that shows candy bar consumption by grade for a particular elementary school for a particular month.

MATERIALS NEEDED:
- Paper
- Pencil or pen
- Ruler
- Set of colored pencils or fine-tip markers

Start by gathering the following data for Greenwood Elementary for the month of October:

CANDY BARS CONSUMED BY GRADE—OCTOBER	
Grade	Candy Bars Consumed
Kindergarten	150
1st Grade	200
2nd Grade	250
3rd Grade	400
4th Grade	125
5th Grade	100

Have your child use the ruler to create a box that will frame your bar chart. Assuming you want to create a horizontal bar chart, have your child write the categories along the left side of the chart, roughly equidistant apart: K, 1st, 2nd, 3rd, 4th, 5th. Remind your child to be sure to leave enough space for the bars, and for spaces between the bars.

Next, using the ruler, your child should create a scale along the bottom of the bar chart. Given the data you're graphing, you might use a scale such as "1" equals 100 candy bars." That would make the largest bar in your chart 4" long. The kindergarten bar will be 1½", the 1st grade bar will be 2", and so on. Have your child color the bars different colors to help set them apart from one another visually. If you'd prefer a smaller bar graph, you can easily reduce the scale. Below is a bar graph representing the candy bar data that uses ½" for every 50 candy bars.

Invite your child to practice creating her own bar chart with other topics as well. She can gather some raw data by asking four or five friends one of the following questions:

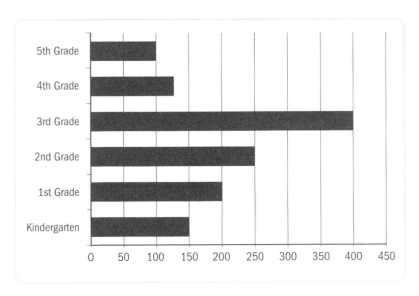

1. How many states have you visited?
2. How many pets have you had in your lifetime?
3. How many musical instruments are in your home?
4. How many cousins do you have?
5. How many times have you flown in an airplane?
6. How many plants are in your home?

Each friend will represent a category in your child's bar chart. Depending on her age and mathematical ability, you may have to help your child create a scale for her chart. Allow her to complete as much of the chart as she can on her own. Remind her to dress up her bar chart by coloring each of the bars a different color.

STEM Words to Know

pictograph

A *pictograph* is a type of graphical display that is very similar to a bar chart. A pictograph uses images or symbols to represent data. For example, suppose you wanted to create a graphic displaying the numbers of cars in each of three automobile categories: gas, electric, and hybrid. You could present your data using a traditional bar chart, or you could use a pictograph in which the bars are replaced by pictures of little cars (each car symbol in your chart might represent 1,000 actual cars, for instance). Like a bar chart, the symbols in a pictograph can be stacked horizontally or vertically.

LEARNING PROBABILITY WITH CARDS AND DICE

People frequently tend to miscalculate the likelihood, or probability, of various events occurring. Some of the rules of probability are complex and best suited for a college-level course or an advanced-level high-school course. But some of the basics of probability can be understood by a student in elementary school. The following activities provide an introduction to some basic aspects of probability theory.

STEM Words to Know

classical probability

Classical probability is one of the more common approaches to calculating probability. The approach applies to situations in which all the outcomes are equally likely. Based on classical probability, the likelihood of a particular event occurring is equal to the number of favorable outcomes divided by the number of total possible outcomes. For instance, if you're rolling a single die the number of possible outcomes is 6. If you're interested in the probability of rolling an even number on the die, there would be 3 favorable outcomes. Thus, using the classical approach, the probability of rolling an even number is $\frac{3}{6}$, or 0.5.

Card Probability

MATERIALS NEEDED:
- Standard deck of playing cards
- Blank sheet of paper
- Pen or pencil

First remove the jokers from the deck so that you have fifty-two total cards. If your child isn't familiar with cards, show her four suits and the various card denominations. Two of the suits are black (clubs and spades) and the other two are red (hearts and diamonds). There are thirteen cards in each suit: the numbers 2 through 10, the three face cards, and one ace. To learn about probability using the card deck, it's best to arrange the cards face up on the table in their respective suits. Explain to your child that you're going to leave the cards face up, but she should imagine that the cards have all been turned face down.

Now ask your child the following questions:

If someone were drawing a card at random (unseen), what is the likelihood that person would choose:

1. A heart
2. A red card
3. A king
4. The king of hearts
5. A king or a heart

Cryptographer

The field of cryptology (or cryptography) involves creating codes and algorithms for encrypting data, as well as devising techniques for breaking codes designed by others. It may all sound like secret spy stuff, and in fact, many people who work in the field are employed by the military. But many non-military organizations also need encrypted data and secure communications, such as banks, credit card companies, and law enforcement agencies. Many cryptographers have graduate training in advanced mathematics or computer science. Cryptographers who work for the military must receive a security clearance before working with classified information.

Some Probability Basics

Probability can be expressed as a fraction, in decimal form, or as a percentage. For example, you might hear the weather forecaster say there's a 40% chance of rain later in the week. The weather forecaster is making a statement about probability.

STEM Q&A

What is the range of probability?

The probability of anything occurring is always somewhere between 0 and 1 (0% and 100%), inclusive. An event can never have a 110% probability of occurring. Probability also can't be negative. There could never be a –15% chance of rain later in the week, for instance.

It should be fairly easy to see that the probability of drawing a heart is $^{13}/_{52}$, since there are 13 hearts and 52 total cards. That, of course, simplifies to $^{1}/_{4}$ or 0.25.

THE SPECIAL RULE OF ADDITION

The probability of drawing a red card will be greater than $^{1}/_{4}$ since there are more red cards in the deck than hearts. One of the basic rules of probability is the *special rule of addition*, which says that the probability of A or B occurring is the same as the probability of A occurring plus the probability of B occurring, as long as A and B are mutually exclusive. In this case, A and B are mutually exclusive because a card can't be both a heart and a diamond—a single card can only belong to one suit. Therefore the probability of drawing a red card is the probability of drawing a heart plus the probability of drawing a diamond, or $^{1}/_{4} + ^{1}/_{4} = ^{1}/_{2}$.

THE GENERAL RULE OF ADDITION

There are 4 kings in the deck, so the probability of drawing a king is $\frac{4}{52}$, which simplifies to $\frac{1}{13}$ or 0.077. Likewise, you can see that the probability of drawing the king of hearts is $\frac{1}{52}$, or 0.01923, since there's only 1 such card in the deck.

STEM Words to Know

complement rule

The complement rule is another useful probability rule. Complementary events are events whose probabilities sum to 1. In a standard deck of cards (sans jokers), drawing a red card and drawing a black card are complementary events. Since you know that the probability of drawing a red card is $\frac{1}{2}$, you instantly know that the probability of drawing a black card is $\frac{1}{2}$, because the two events are complementary.

The special rule of addition doesn't work for calculating the likelihood of drawing a king or a heart. If you've followed along with the entire activity so far, you've already seen that the probability of drawing a heart is $\frac{13}{52}$. Following the special rule of addition, the probability of drawing a king plus the probability of drawing a heart would be $\frac{4}{52} + \frac{13}{52} = \frac{17}{52}$. But that answer is not quite correct. With the cards spread out in front of you face up, you can see that there are 13 hearts and 3 kings that aren't hearts. So the likelihood of drawing a king or a heart is actually $\frac{16}{52}$.

The reason the special rule of addition doesn't work in this case is because the category "king" and the category "heart" are not mutually exclusive. There is overlap between the two categories because the king of hearts belongs to both categories. When A and B aren't mutually exclusive, you have to rely on another probability rule, the *general rule of addition*.

The general rule of addition says that the probability of A or B occurring is the probability of A occurring plus the probability of

B occurring, minus the probability of A and B both occurring. Thus the probability of drawing the king of hearts is equal to the probability of drawing a king plus the probability of drawing a heart, less the probability of drawing the king of hearts, or:

$$^{4}/_{52} + {^{13}/_{52}} - {^{1}/_{52}} = {^{16}/_{52}}$$

Extending the Activity

There are several ways you can extend the probability playing card activity. Ask your child to calculate the probability for each of the following scenarios.

If someone were drawing a card at random (unseen), what is the likelihood that person would choose:

1. A club or spade
2. A face card
3. An ace
4. The ace of spades
5. An ace or a spade

Encourage your child to try using the special rule of addition to solve #1 and the general rule of addition to solve #5.

Another way to extend the activity is to choose one of the probabilities related to the card deck and test it out. For example, the probability of drawing a red card is ½. Invite your child to turn the cards face down, shuffle them, draw a card at random, and record whether it's a red or black card. Repeat the shuffle and draw twenty times or so, making sure to replace the card after each draw. Consult the record and see if a red card was drawn approximately half the time. Repeat the experiment for another of the card probabilities.

Dice Probability

Games of chance are all about probability. In fact, the first rules of probability were devised because a seventeenth-century French nobleman wanted to gain a better understanding of a particular casino game. His appeal to mathematician Blaise Pascal, and Pascal's subsequent correspondence with mathematician Pierre de Fermat, led to the birth of probability theory.

Earlier in this chapter, two basic rules of probability—the special rule of addition and the general rule of addition—were introduced using a card activity. Here, another important probability rule is introduced using a simple dice activity.

MATERIALS NEEDED:

- Pair of dice
- Blank paper
- Pen or pencil

PROBABILITY FOR A SINGLE THROW

Start with a single die. Ask your child what her favorite number is between 1 and 6. Then ask if she can figure out the likelihood of rolling her favorite number on a die. It should be fairly easy for her to see that the probability of rolling any number between 1 and 6 is ⅙. This is a simple calculation based on the notion of classical probability.

STEM Words to Know

empirical probability

Classical probability is only one approach that is used to calculate the likelihood of various events occurring. *Empirical probability* relies on using information from the past to determine probabilities for future events. For example, suppose that you have a mouse that, over the course of a month, appears in your house 3 mornings out of 4. The probability of the mouse appearing on any particular future morning would be ¾, or 0.75, based on the notion of empirical probability.

PROBABILITY FOR MULTIPLE THROWS

It's easy to calculate the likelihood of rolling any particular number on one throw of a die. But what about multiple throws? Suppose your child said her favorite number on a die was 5. The probability of rolling a 5 on a single throw of the die is ⅙. What's the probability of throwing two 5s in a row?

STEM Words to Know

independent events

Two events are considered *independent events* if the occurrence of one has no effect on the probability of the other occurring. For instance, the probability of drawing a black card from a standard 52-card deck is ½. If you draw a black card and subsequently put it back in the deck, the probability of drawing a black card a second time remains ½. The first draw and the second draw would be independent events. However, if you draw a black card and keep it out of the deck, the probability of drawing a second black card is no longer ½. In this case, the first draw and the second draw are not independent because the first draw impacts the probability of the second draw.

Neither the special rule nor the general rule of addition will help answer that question. Both of those additive rules apply to situations in which you want to find the probability of A *or* B occurring. Calculating the probability of throwing two 5s on a die is about finding the probability of A *and* B occurring. Specifically, you want to know the probability of throwing a 5 and then another 5 on a die. For a problem like this, you'll want to use a basic probability rule known as the *special rule of multiplication*. The special rule of multiplication is used when you want to find the likelihood of A *and* B occurring. It's important to note that the special rule of multiplication only works in cases where A and B are independent events.

The special rule of multiplication is easy to use. It states that if A and B are independent events, the probability of A and B both occurring is equal to the probability of A occurring times the probability of B occurring.

The probability of rolling a 5 on the first roll of a die is ⅙. Think of that as event A. The probability of rolling a 5 on the second roll of a die—event B—is also ⅙. So the probability of rolling two 5s in a row is (⅙) × (⅙) = 1/36.

With paper, a pen, and a little time, you can prove to yourself that the special rule of multiplication works. Invite your child to write out on a sheet of paper all the possible arrangements of two throws of a die. She can actually draw pictures of dice with dots, if it helps her visualize the problem.

One possible arrangement is a 1 on the first throw of the die, and a 1 on the second throw. Another possible arrangement is a 1 on the first throw and a 2 on the second throw, and so on. When your child finishes drawing out the possibilities, there should be 36 different arrangements depicted on the page. How many of those arrangements include a 5 on the first roll and a 5 on the second roll? Only 1 of them does: 1 out of 36 possible arrangements. But this is a somewhat time-consuming way to solve the problem. The special rule of multiplication yields the answer much more quickly.

Note that when the events are not independent, the calculation of probability becomes more involved. A discussion of probability in those situations is better suited for an advanced-level class in high school or college.

Extending the Activity

Ask your child to calculate the probability of each of the following events. Remind her to use the special rule of multiplication where it's appropriate.

Find the probability of each of the following events:

- Rolling an even number on a single die
- Rolling two 5s in a row on a die
- Rolling three 5s in a row on a die
- Flipping a coin and having it turn up heads
- Flipping two heads in a row on a coin

The special rule of multiplication works for any number of independent events. The probability of A and B and C occurring can be found using the special rule of multiplication as long as the three events are independent. So the probability of rolling three 5s in a row on a die is ($\frac{1}{6}$) × ($\frac{1}{6}$) × ($\frac{1}{6}$), which equals $\frac{1}{216}$, or 0.00463.

THE BIRTHDAY PROBLEM

The Birthday Problem is a well-known scenario in statistics that is fun to test out in real life. The problem begins with a simple question: If you have 23 people in a room, what's the likelihood that 2 of them share the same birthday? When considering the question, ignore February 29, which of course doesn't come around every year. Also, only consider the month and day of birth, not the year.

You might assume it would be very unlikely for 2 or more individuals in a group of 23 to have the same birthday, but actually the probability is higher than most people would expect. The probability is greater than 50 percent that 2 or more people in a group of 23 will share a birthday. The statistical explanation, which is somewhat advanced, is presented here:

Using the special multiplication rule mentioned previously, you can calculate the probability that 2 people in a group of 23 do *not* share a birthday as follows:

$$\frac{365}{365} \times \frac{364}{365} \times \frac{363}{365} \times \ldots \times \frac{343}{365} = 0.4927$$

This expression states that the probability of the 2nd person not sharing a birthday with the 1st person is $\frac{364}{365}$, the likelihood of the 3rd person not sharing a birthday with the 1st or 2nd person is $\frac{363}{365}$, and so on.

If the probability of 2 people in 23 not sharing a birthday is 0.4927, then the probability of 2 of them sharing a birthday can be calculated as follows:

1 – 0.4927 = 0.5073 or 50.7 percent

The Birthday Problem is a great activity to try out at a gathering of 23 or more people. But it can also be done as a travel game, even if you're not traveling with 22 other passengers. There are a couple of ways you can approach the Birthday Problem as a travel game. If you have, say, 4 people in the car, you can begin with the birthdays of those 4 individuals. Then if each of the 4 can think of 5 other birthdays of people he or she knows, you'll have a sample of at least 24 birthdays. Another way you can approach the problem as a travel game is to have someone (*not* the driver) text people and ask their birthdays. If you repeat this activity several times, asking different subjects for their birthdays, you should have a birthday match on roughly every other trial. Incidentally, if you ask 57 different people their birthdays, there's a 99 percent likelihood that 2 of the 57 will share a birthday. The Birthday Problem may seem like a paradox, but it has a solid statistical explanation.

Economist

Many people confuse economists with stockbrokers, but the two careers are very different from each other. Economists gather and utilize data to solve economic problems. Lots of economists never deal with stocks or bonds as part of their work. An economist may work with a company to help it set prices for a new line of products. An economist might help a local government determine the optimal, or best, tax rate for a new hotel tax. Economists are employed in a wide array of industries, with a large number concentrated in the banking and finance industries. Economists also work for universities, and in all levels of government. Most professional economists earn graduate degrees in economics, but some entry-level jobs are available for individuals with bachelor's degrees in economics.

HOW MANY ZEROS ARE IN A QUADRILLION?

The zero is undoubtedly one of the greatest inventions in the history of mankind. If you doubt that statement, just take a moment to think about what our number system would be like without it. Instead of having ten digits—0, 1, 2, 3, 4, 5, 6, 7, 8, and 9—we would need a unique digit for every number used. If you counted 100 of something, you couldn't write it as a 1 followed by two zeros. You would have to write it using unique symbols. Perhaps it would be written as 1ğẑ or 1¢ϕ. Can you image how complicated our number system would be without the zero?

The Importance of Place Value

The number system most commonly used today is known as the decimal or base 10 system. The value of a particular digit depends on its *place value*, or where it lies in the number. The place to the immediate left of the decimal is the ones place. Immediately left of that is the tens place. Left of that is the hundreds place, then the thousands place, then the ten thousands place, and so on.

STEM Words to Know

googol

One famous large number is the *googol*, which is 10 raised to the hundredth power, or 10^{100}. Written out, a googol would be 1 followed by 100 zeros. The googol doesn't have any special significance in mathematics, but it did inspire the name of an extremely well-known search engine.

To the immediate right of the decimal is the tenths place. To the right of that is the hundredths place. Right of that is the thousandths place, then the ten thousandths place, and so on. Of course, when it comes to dollar amounts, the number is usually rounded to the hundredths decimal place.

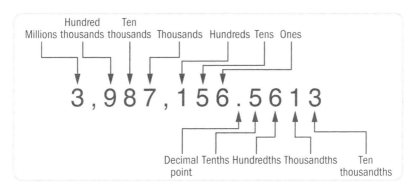

Decimal Place Value Chart

The zero serves as a placeholder. For example, if you write the number one hundred and one in digits you'll write 101. The 1 in the hundreds place indicates 1 hundred, the 0 in the tens place indicates 0 tens, and the 1 in the ones place indicates 1 one. Without the zero you would have to write 11, but that wouldn't carry the same value as 101. With the zero as a placeholder in the tens place, you know that you're dealing with a number whose value is at least one hundred.

The Place Value Game

Try this simple game that will help reinforce your child's understanding of place value in the decimal or base 10 number system.

MATERIALS NEEDED:

- Blank paper
- Black marker or felt-tip pen
- Pencil and eraser
- Pair of dice
- Watch or timer

Using the black marker, create spaces by drawing short blank lines on the paper for the millions place through the ten thousandths place. Be sure to include the decimal, which will serve as a reference point. When you're finished, you should have seven spaces to the left of the decimal point and four spaces to the right of the decimal. You can use the place value chart provided as a guide.

After you've created your game board, randomly choose digits to populate the spaces. (You might want to use a pencil so you can erase the numbers later and reuse the game board.) You can roll a single die repeatedly and use the resulting numbers to populate the spaces, or you can use an online random number generator, or you can simply pick numbers from thin air. When you're finished, you should have all eleven spaces filled with a number.

Accountant

Accountants prepare and analyze financial statements. Essentially they help organizations keep their financial records in order. Some accountants specialize in preparing tax returns. Others in the field work as auditors, meaning that they're hired to make sure a company's financial statements comply with the law. Many accountants also earn a special certification, such as CPA (certified public accountant) or CMA (certified management accountant).

To begin the game, have your child roll a single die and note the resulting number. He should look for that on the game board. Be sure to set the timer—he has ten seconds from the time he rolls the die to identify the place value of the number on the die. For example, suppose he rolls a 2 on the die. He should look for a 2 on the game board. Suppose there is a 2 in the thousands place. He has until the timer runs out to say "thousands place." If he does so within the time limit, he wins the round. If the number on the die appears in more than one place on the game board, he may choose one place value to identify.

If your child rolls a 2 and there are no 2s on the game board, then have him roll again. He should alternate between rolling a single die and the pair so that values over 6 will be included in the game. When he rolls the pair of dice he should promptly add the dots on the dice and look for that number on the game board. If the numbers on the dice sum to 10, 11, or 12, then he may disregard the dice and just identify the place value of any number on the board he wishes. Play until your child has successfully identified the place value of each digit on the game board, then erase the numbers and try again with new numbers. You can also consider trying an extension of the game where you add a dollar sign on the left side and only carry the decimals to the hundredths place. You might find that your child has an easier time identifying place values when the numbers are dollar amounts.

Really Big Numbers

What's the biggest possible number in the universe? The truth is there's no limit on how large (or how small) a number can get. Most people know that a million comes after a thousand, and that a billion comes after a million. Lots of people also know that a trillion comes after a billion. But what comes after a trillion? Take a look at the following list to find out.

REALLY BIG NUMBERS:
- A million has 6 zeros: 1,000,000
- A billion has 9 zeros: 1,000,000,000
- A trillion has 12 zeros: 1,000,000,000,000
- A quadrillion has 15 zeros: 1,000,000,000,000,000
- A quintillion has 18 zeros: 1,000,000,000,000,000,000

And the numbers get bigger (and the names stranger) than a sextillion. To cite a few examples, an undecillion has 36 zeros, a quattuordecillion has 45 zeros, and a novemdecillion has 60 zeros!

MONEY'S VALUE OVER TIME

One of the best-kept secrets about money is how its value changes over time. Actually it's not really a secret, but many people seem to ignore or overlook the concept of the time value of money. The younger you are when you learn about the time value of money, the greater your opportunity to take advantage of it.

Simple Interest

When you keep your money in the bank—in a savings account or certain other types of accounts—the bank pays you for keeping it there. The money the bank pays you is known as *interest*. Interest is expressed in percentage terms. Just to make the math straightforward, suppose the bank is paying interest of 5% annually to hold your money. Note that the bank doesn't just park your money; the bank actually uses your money to make loans to borrowers who are looking to buy houses, cars, businesses, and other big-ticket items.

STEM Q&A

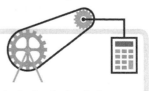

Are there shortcuts for figuring out the ending year balance?

Yes, if you have an interest rate. Simply multiply the beginning balance by 1 + the annual interest rate in decimal terms to arrive at the ending account balance. Using the example given, $100 × 1.05 = $105.

Suppose you put $100 in your account at the beginning of the year. How much would you have in your account at the end of the year, assuming you didn't make any other deposits or any withdrawals during the year? Your end-of-year balance would be equal to your beginning balance plus the interest you earned over the year. If the bank pays 5% interest on a yearly basis, the amount of interest earned over the year would be $100 × 5%, or $5. (Note that 5% in decimal form is 0.05, so 100 × 0.05 = 5.) Your balance at the end of the year would therefore be $100 + $5 = $105.

Compound Interest

The beautiful thing about interest paid on bank deposits is that it keeps on accumulating as long as there's money in the account. Not only does the bank pay interest on the initial amount you deposited, but the bank also pays interest on the interest your account previously earned. This is known as *compound interest*, and it makes saving money a lot of fun.

For example, at the end of year two, you would have $110.25 in your account, assuming you didn't make any additional deposits or any withdrawals in the second year. That amount is found by multiplying $105 by 5% (or 0.05) and adding that value—which is the interest earned in the second year—to your account balance at the end of the first year.

$105 × 5% = $5.25. And $105 + $5.25 = $110.25

Take a few moments and help your child calculate what the balance will be at the end year three, again assuming that no additional deposits and no withdrawals are made during the third year. If she understands decimal math, she should be able to figure out that the account balance at the end of year three will be approximately $115.76 (calculated by $110.25 × 1.05).

A Formula for Calculating Compound Interest

Suppose you left the $100 in the bank for ten years, and the bank paid 5% interest per year. You could calculate the ending balance by hand using the method already outlined. There is a faster way to arrive at the answer, but it requires a bit more math ability. The formula for calculating compound interest for interest compounded annually is:

$$PV \times (1 + r)^n = FV$$

where PV is the present value or starting account balance, r is the yearly interest rate (in decimal form), n is the number of periods, and FV is the future value, or the ending balance of the account. At the end of ten years, your account that started with $100 will have a balance of:

$$\$100 \times (1.05)^{10} = \$162.89$$

It's interesting to note that after fourteen years, the account will have a balance of approximately $198. Within fourteen years, your money will have nearly doubled, thanks to the magic of compound interest. Note that the formula becomes slightly more complex if the interest is compounded semiannually, quarterly, monthly, or daily.

A Savings Plan

Perhaps after explaining compound interest to your child, you can help her create a savings plan. There's a formula that determines how much money you would have in an account if you were to save a set amount on a regular basis. Suppose your child managed to save $1,200 per year, depositing that amount at the end of each year, for forty years. At a 5% annual interest rate, after forty years, she would have about $144,960 in her account. Without interest payments she would only have $1,200 × 40 = $48,000. See the difference compound interest makes over time? People who begin saving while they're young and save consistently over a number of years can accumulate a large amount of money.

Compound interest problems can get complicated, depending on the particulars of the problem. There are financial calculators, software programs, and online calculators to help solve more advanced problems. The main purpose of this section is to highlight the concept of the time value of money and to introduce some of the basic math involved in these important financial calculations.

Financial Analyst

Companies like to be wise with their money, just as most individuals do. Financial analysts help companies invest their money wisely. Financial analysts—who are sometimes called investment analysts or securities analysts—work for banks, mutual funds, insurance companies, and other firms. As part of their job, financial analysts must stay up to date on the latest financial news. Many of them become experts in a particular industry, or in a handful of industries. To get a job as a financial analyst you need at least a bachelor's degree in finance, accounting, business administration, statistics, or some related field. A graduate degree may be required for higher-level positions. The demand for financial analysts is expected to grow at a faster-than-average rate over the coming years.

Extra Practice

To be sure your child understands basic time value of money calculations, invite her to try the following problems.

Calculate the future value, or ending account balance, in each of the following scenarios:

1. The beginning balance is $1,000, the yearly interest rate is 4%, the number of years is 4.
2. The beginning balance is $1,000, the yearly interest rate is 1%, the number of years is 4.
3. The beginning balance is $1,000, the yearly interest rate is 4%, the number of years is 12.
4. The beginning balance is $1,000, the yearly interest rate is 8%, the number of years is 4.
5. The beginning balance is $2,000, the yearly interest rate is 4%, the number of years is 4.

ANSWERS:

1. $\$1,000 \times (1.04)^4 = \$1,169.86$
2. $\$1,000 \times (1.01)^4 = \$1,040.60$
3. $\$1,000 \times (1.04)^{12} = \$1,601.03$
4. $\$1,000 \times (1.08)^4 = \$1,360.49$
5. $\$2,000 \times (1.04)^4 = \$2,339.72$

Software Engineer

Sometimes people use the terms *computer programmer* and *software engineer* (or *software developer*) interchangeably, but there is a difference. Programmers usually have great coding skills, but they may not always operate with the big picture in mind. Software engineers work with the people who will be using the application, and they strive to make sure the final product does what it's supposed to do. A computer programmer may work on a particular part of an application; a software engineer makes sure that the different component parts fit together in the end and that the program works as intended. Computer programming is more of an individual activity while software engineering requires more teamwork. Demand for software engineers is strong and is expected to remain strong in the coming years.

CHAPTER 8

GETTING A HEAD START IN STEM

If your child is really interested in working in a STEM field some day, it's a good idea for her to begin learning all she can about various fields before she enters college. Would she rather work in one of the life sciences or in computer science? Perhaps she'd prefer a career in astrophysics or engineering. One way she can begin to learn about a particular STEM field is by taking an online enrichment class related to that field. There are also numerous STEM summer camps and afterschool workshops available if she prefers hands-on learning. If she really wants to understand the day-in-day-out activities involved in a particular career, she should consider job shadowing—spending part of a workday with a person employed in the field she'd like to learn about. This chapter lists dozens of extracurricular STEM-based educational opportunities for young learners, including summer camps, afterschool classes, and online classes. In addition, the chapter offers some guidelines and suggestions to consider if you and your child would like to set up a STEM-related job-shadowing experience.

STEM Camps and Enrichment Classes

In every major city, as well as in many smaller communities, opportunities abound for kids to engage in STEM subjects outside the classroom. These enrichment opportunities take the form of afterschool classes, summer camps, winter break camps, and spring break camps. The following providers of STEM enrichment programs share some similarities, but each approaches its mission from a slightly different angle.

Mad Science Group

www.madscience.org

Mad Science is a Canadian-based franchise company that offers science-based summer camps, afterschool enrichment classes, in-school field trips, and birthday programs for kids from preschool through middle school. Mad Science operates in hundreds of locations throughout North America and around the world. Mad Science offers programs relating to nearly every area of science. The company's programs include titles such as Science of Magic, Red Hot Robots, Fun Physics, Slime Time, Crazy Chemworks, Techno Safari, and Planet Rock!

Bricks 4 Kidz

www.bricks4kidz.com

Bricks 4 Kidz is one of the many companies offering enrichment classes and summer camps for kids focusing on engineering, architecture, and robotics. Bricks 4 Kidz has franchises across North America and in numerous countries overseas. Bricks 4 Kidz utilizes kits from LEGO Education along with proprietary builds and other materials for its classes.

Engineering for Kids

http://engineeringforkids.com

Engineering for Kids is another company that offers a suite of programs designed to introduce kids up to age fourteen to STEM-related subjects. With over 100 locations in the United States and several locations overseas, Engineering for Kids offers camps, afterschool classes, and birthday parties. Engineering for Kids' afterschool and evening classes are focused on a specific discipline of engineering such as civil, electrical, or aerospace engineering.

Robotics Engineer and Robotics Technician

There was a time when robots existed only in science fiction stories. Now robots are a part of everyday life. They've become especially important in some industries, such as heavy manufacturing. If not for the work of robotics engineers and technicians, robots would still only exist in sci-fi books and movies. Robotics engineers design and build robots, along with the systems that control the robots. To do their jobs, robotics engineers must acquire much of the same knowledge as mechanical engineers, along with programming knowledge. To work as a robotics engineer, a person typically needs a bachelor's degree in robotics engineering or a related field. Robotics technicians help test robots during the design process, and operate and maintain robots after they've been installed. Most robotics technicians complete a two-year technical program before entering the field.

All About Learning

www.allaboutlearning.co

All About Learning provides STEM-related enrichment classes and summer camps for kids from kindergarten through eighth grade utilizing LEGO Education kits and LEGO elements. Representative programs include Gears and Gadgets, FUN-gineering, Collision Cars, Video Game Making, and Journey Into Space.

IMACS

www.imacs.org

For students in grades one to twelve, IMACS (the Institute for Mathematics and Computer Science) offers afterschool, weekend, and homeschool classes as well as a summer camp. Working solo and in teams, IMACS students learn how to think logically and creatively while having fun with games, puzzles, stories, and other engaging activities. The IMACS Hi-Tech Summer Camp program engages students with logic puzzles, computer programming, virtual robotics, and electronics. Advanced students entering grades nine to twelve may also enroll in IMACS's university-level programs in mathematical logic and computer science.

Play-Well TEKnologies
www.play-well.org

Play-Well TEKnologies offers LEGO-inspired engineering classes, summer camps, and birthday party programs for kids from kindergarten through eighth grade. Play-Well TEKnologies's classes and camps are available in over 2,000 locations nationwide.

Mobile App Developer

With people relying more on their smartphones all the time, mobile apps are more relevant than ever. Mobile app developers are essentially software developers who specialize in creating applications for mobile devices. Whether an app is produced for some practical purpose or for pure entertainment, someone has to dream up the app and then create the coding that makes the app a reality. A bachelor's degree in computer science is excellent preparation for a career in mobile app development. Specialized training programs also exist that teach the programming skills necessary for app development. Many mobile app developers specialize in a particular platform (e.g., iOS or Android). Demand for mobile app developers is only expected to increase as demand for interesting new smartphone apps continues to rise across the globe.

iD Tech

www.idtech.com

California-based iD Tech is a provider of tech-based summer day camps and overnight camps for students ages six to seventeen. iD Tech's camps are offered at some of the most prestigious college campuses in the country. The company's camps cover topics such as programming, video game design, 3D modeling, robotics, and digital arts. In addition, iD Tech has a unique all-girls' program in place for girls ages ten to fifteen called Alexa Café.

Digital Media Academy

www.digitalmediaacademy.org

In addition to offering continuing studies classes for adults, Digital Media Academy (DMA) provides tech-based summer camps for young people ages six to eighteen. Based in several university campuses around the country, DMA's youth camps cover such topics as programming and app development, robotics and engineering, 3D modeling and animation, filmmaking and visual effects, and game design and development.

Additional Providers

A number of organizations offer STEM-related camps or classes on a regional basis. Emagination, Snapology, i2 Camp, and Ideaventions are just a few. Also, many community colleges offer STEM-related summer camps and spring break camps for elementary and high-school students.

Online STEM Classes

A number of companies and organizations offer online STEM classes for kids. Some of the classes are targeted at homeschoolers and offer a complete science curriculum. Others are supplemental in nature. Online classes are especially good for kids interested in coding since coding isn't taught in every school. Some of the options for online STEM classes are listed here.

Supercharged Science
www.superchargedscience.com

Created by a former NASA scientist, Supercharged Science offers a complete online science program for homeschoolers. The program teaches science using a combination of videos, live tele-classes, reading, and exercises. It's designed so that parents don't have to know science themselves in order for their kids to participate. Supercharged Science offers curricula for grades one through twelve. Its services are available on a monthly subscription basis.

Time4Learning
www.time4learning.com

Time4Learning's curriculum covers kindergarten to twelfth grade and is appropriate for homeschool, afterschool, and summer skill building. The sixth-grade through twelfth-grade curricula are correlated to state standards.

Real Science 4 Kids
http://gravitaspublications.com

Real Science 4 Kids is a publication-based science program with some online classes available in the core subjects.

Youth Digital
www.youthdigital.com

Youth Digital offers technology courses for kids ages eight to fourteen through a highly interactive learning platform. Youth Digital offers courses in Java coding, digital illustration, 3D animation, game design, and app design.

Tynker
www.tynker.com

Tynker offers programming education through interactive self-paced courses and game-based activities. In additional to grade-based curricula for schools, Tynker offers classes for individual students as well as instructor-led summer camps and afterschool clubs.

Homeschool Programming, Inc

www.homeschoolprogramming.com

Homeschool Programming, Inc., founded by homeschooling parents, offers online programming courses for kids in fourth grade and up. Its kid track includes classes in beginning and advanced web design, as well as Windows programming and game programming. The company's teen track features classes in Windows programming, game programming, and Java and Android programming.

Gamestar Mechanic

http://gamestarmechanic.com

Gamestar Mechanic offers game-based classes and quests that teach users how to create their own video games. The site also allows users to publish their games and join an online community of game designers.

Quick Study Labs

www.quickstudylabs.com

Quick Study Labs offers electronics classes for kids ages eight and up. In addition to electronics, the company offers online courses in robotics and green technology.

Other Online Learning Resources

Online classes aren't the only resources available on the Internet for learning about STEM subjects. Other web-based tools exist that offer kids the opportunity to learn coding, build websites, create animations, and discover other intriguing applications. Several exceptional sites are listed here.

Scratch

www.scratch.mit.edu

Scratch is a site developed and maintained at MIT for the purpose of teaching basic programming concepts to youths ages eight to sixteen. A visual programming language, Scratch allows users to build games, animations, interactive stories, and art. Scratch is free to download.

Code.org

https://code.org

Code.org is a nonprofit dedicated to expanding participation in computer science by making it available in more schools. Code.org has some heavy-hitting corporate partners, such as Amazon, Facebook, Microsoft, and Google. Its online platform, Code Studio (https://studio.code.org), offers several free tutorials and courses.

Stencyl

www.stencyl.com

Stencyl is an online game-creation software that allows users to design games and publish them to iOS, Android, Flash, Windows, Mac, and Linux. Stencyl utilizes freemium-style pricing, with a free starter version available.

Alice

www.alice.org

Alice is a 3D programming environment that allows users to create animations for videos or interactive games. Designed to be a student's first exposure to object-oriented programming, Alice is free to download and use.

Code Monster

www.crunchzilla.com/code-monster

Code Monster is a free online tutorial designed to teach programming basics to kids. Code Monster offers a simple introduction to elementary programming concepts such as variables, functions, loops, and conditionals.

Codecademy

www.codecademy.com

Codecademy offers a fun, social introduction to programming for higher-level students. Students learn programming skills and

JavaScript in an interactive manner, receiving feedback as they code and earning badges as they reach certain milestones.

CoderDojo

https://coderdojo.com

CoderDojo is a worldwide network of independent community-based youth programming clubs. CoderDojo club members learn to code and to develop programs, games, and apps in a fun, social environment. CoderDojo clubs are led by volunteers and are free to participants.

Web Developer

Nearly every business, nonprofit organization, and government agency has a website. With so many places to go on the Internet, how can an organization make its site stand out from the crowd? That's the basic responsibility of a web developer. Simply stated, web developers design and build websites, striving to make the sites as attractive and as user-friendly as possible. You may already have some experience with website design. It's not difficult to create a basic website using a template, but building a larger site with advanced functionality requires more know-how. Web developers typically possess some programming skills along with graphic design skills. Some companies seek out web developers who've earned a bachelor's degree, while other organizations are willing to hire candidates with associate's degrees. Of course, there's nothing to prevent you from learning web development on your own and going into business for yourself. According to the Bureau of Labor Statistics, about one in seven web developers are self-employed.

Made with Code

www.madewithcode.com

Made with Code is one of Google's initiatives to inspire girls to get involved in coding. The site features introductory coding projects for girls who've never tried coding, as well as advanced resources. The site also features an online community for girl coders around the world.

Job Shadowing

Job shadowing isn't a new idea. "Take Our Daughters and Sons to Work Day" is a familiar concept to most people. Job shadowing expands the concept of "Take Our Daughters and Sons to Work Day" beyond the workplaces of a child's own parents. It creates possibilities for a child to visit any workplace and learn about any career in which he or she has an interest. Job shadowing is a useful way to expose a young person to any career field, but it's particularly useful in motivating kids to pursue STEM careers.

Job Shadowing in the STEM Fields

A job-shadowing experience isn't the same as an internship, nor is it a field trip. Typically it involves an individual student following, or shadowing, a professional through his regular workday. The point is for the student to get a good idea of the daily activities a particular job entails. Most job-shadowing experiences will also include some time for the student to ask questions.

Job shadowing is a good idea for any career field, but it's an especially good way to expose young people to various STEM careers. Most would agree that STEM fields are underrepresented on TV and in movies. Unless a child has family members directly employed in STEM fields, the child will likely have little knowledge of careers in those fields.

A study published in the *Journal of Applied Communication Research* found that high-school students tend to become more motivated to enter STEM careers after having visited workplaces where such jobs take place. Job shadowing is often done for students at the college and high-school levels, but younger students can also benefit from such experiences. Some employers actually believe middle school is the best time to plant the seed in a young person's mind with respect to STEM. Following are some suggestions for finding job-shadowing opportunities in the STEM fields.

Finding Job-Shadowing Opportunities

Although many people are beginning to recognize the value of job shadowing in promoting the STEM fields, there aren't yet any broad-based nationwide programs set up to connect interested students with job-shadowing opportunities. Most existing job-shadowing programs are local or regional in scope. Companies that heavily rely on STEM skills, such as Boeing, Procter & Gamble, and Lockheed Martin have in the past offered job-shadowing opportunities in some of the cities where their facilities are located. NASA has also offered some job-shadowing opportunities in the past; however, the agency's educational programming will always be subject to budgetary considerations.

You can start seeking out a STEM job-shadowing arrangement for your child by first consulting your school's guidance counselor. You might be pleasantly surprised and discover that your child's school already has a program in place, or at least an available list of job-shadowing resources. If the counselor has no resources to offer, take your search to the Internet. Start with companies and other organizations in your area that are known to employ STEM workers. Likely candidates include technology firms, research facilities, manufacturing companies, and hospitals. Contact those companies' HR departments and ask about the possibility of setting up a job shadow for your child. If you have a community college in your area, you can contact individual department chairs in the STEM fields and ask for ideas. Most community colleges have strong ties to STEM employers in their service areas. If you know an individual employee, even only casually, consider approaching that person directly. A sample letter (or e-mail) proposing a job shadow is included at the end of this section.

Virtual Job Shadowing

In an ideal world, your child's school would have a rich job-shadowing program in place for its students. If your child's school hasn't established a job-shadowing program, there may be practical reasons why it hasn't happened. First, if you live in a rural area, there may be limited opportunities for such arrangements. Also, safety concerns may prevent some companies from offering job-shadowing arrangements, particularly to younger children. As an alternative to on-the-ground shadowing, you could consider setting up a virtual experience for your child.

A number of websites provide virtual job-shadowing experiences for students, such as VirtualJobShadow.com. The site's resources are appropriate for students from middle school through college. JobShadow.com offers interviews with individuals in many different career fields, including a number of STEM fields. Although the site doesn't offer true job shadowing—the interviews are written, with no accompanying video—JobShadow .com's resources are available for free. Other sites featuring career videos include America's Career InfoNet (www.careeronestop.org), MyPlan.com, and JobsTVnews.com.

Getting the Most Out of a Job-Shadowing Experience

Before the job-shadowing visit, check ahead (or have your child check ahead) to find out what clothing is appropriate for the visit. It's also a good idea to find out ahead of time whether it's acceptable for your child to ask questions during the visit, or whether questions should be saved for a separate interview. Encourage your child to take notes during the visit, but not to let note-taking distract her from fully absorbing the experience. Reflecting on the job-shadowing experience following the visit, either in writing or using an audio recorder, is something else your child may wish to consider. Also, don't forget to encourage your child to write a thank-you note to the individual or individuals who hosted the job shadow.

Sample Job-Shadowing Letter of Request

Dear (*Job-Shadowing Prospect's Name*):

I am writing to you about a potential job-shadowing arrangement. Currently I'm a student at (*Name of School*), and I'm very much interested in exploring (*Name of Career Field*) as a possible career path. After studying all the material I can find online and in the library related to (*Name of Career Field*), I'm eager to learn more. Your name was given to me by (*School Counselor or Source of Prospect's Name*) as a person who would likely have some valuable insights to share.

If you're able to work it into your busy schedule, I would greatly appreciate the opportunity to shadow you for part of a day as you perform your usual work duties. I would remain quiet while I observe you working, unless you invite me to ask questions during the job shadowing.

Additionally, I would like to ask if I may interview you at the end of my visit, so that I may ask any questions that occur to me during the shadowing. I promise to keep the interview as brief as possible.

I understand that this is a big request, but I would be forever grateful for the opportunity to learn about the field firsthand from a professional such as you. I'm willing to do the visit at whatever time best suits your schedule.

You can reach me in the afternoons and early evenings at (*Your Phone Number*) or anytime by e-mail at (*Your E-mail Address or Parent's E-mail Address*). I look forward to your response, and I very much look forward to the possibility of visiting with you in the near future.

Thank you for your time and consideration.

Sincerely,
(*Your Name*)

P.S. If you're not able to accommodate my visit, but you know of another professional in the area who possibly can, I would greatly appreciate a referral to that person.

APPENDIX A

STEM CAREER WEBSITES FOR KIDS

AIBS

www.aibs.org/careers/

A site chock-full of information for students interested in careers in biology, from the American Institute of Biological Sciences.

Be an Engineer

www.beanengineer.com

Sponsored by ExxonMobil, this site offers stories from and about real engineers in addition to information about various engineering fields.

Biotech Careers

www.biotech-careers.org

A site from Bio-Link providing information for students interested in biotech careers, including videos, on-the-job photos, articles, and internship resources.

Careers in Chemistry

www.acs.org/content/acs/en/careers.html

Sponsored by the American Chemical Society, this site features descriptions of a variety of different careers in chemistry, along with numerous professional resources.

Choosing a STEM Career

www.pbslearningmedia.org/resource/wpsu09-stemcareers.text
.lpchoosingSTEMcareer/choosing-a-stem-career/

A multimedia collection of resources from PBS Learning Media, including videos, articles, and worksheets. The site's resources are aimed at students in grades six to twelve.

Computing Careers

http://computingcareers.acm.org

A site from the Association for Computing Machinery offering information on computing degrees and careers, along with computing news.

Cool Science Careers

www.coolsciencecareers.rice.edu

An interesting interactive site from the Center for Technology in Teaching and Learning at Rice University, offering the Profession Pathfinder game, which matches users with science careers based on interests.

Discover Engineering

www.discovere.org

A community focused on encouraging students to pursue engineering careers; includes an engineering career outlook and information on various engineering fields.

Engineer Girl

www.engineergirl.org

A site offering resources to encourage girls to pursue engineering careers.

Engineering, Go for It!

www.egfi-k12.org

Associated with the American Society for Engineering Education (ASEE), Engineering, Go for It! offers lots of advice and interesting information related to careers in engineering.

Gotta Have IT

www.ncwit.org/resources/gotta-have-it

A site of the National Center for Women & Information Technology associated with an educational kit for a K-to-12 audience. The kit, which promotes IT careers, is for all students, but is aimed especially at young girls.

IEEE Spark

http://spark.ieee.org

An online publication aimed at students ages 14 to 18, IEEE Spark offers career profiles, college prep tips, learning activities, news articles, comics, and more. Published by the Institute of Electrical and Electronics Engineers, the site's goal is to inspire young people to pursue careers in technology and engineering.

LifeWorks

www.nihlifeworks.org

An interactive career exploration site aimed at middle- and high-school students, offering detailed information on more than 100 careers in the medical field.

Social Science Careers

www.socialsciencecareers.org

An online guide to careersPleae in the social sciences, including articles and information on degree programs.

STEMCareer

http://stemcareer.com/students

A site with tons of resources related to STEM careers, colleges, internships, and self-learning websites.

STEM-Works

www.stem-works.com

STEM-Works offers a plethora of resources for parents, teachers, and STEM professionals. The site also offers activities and information on STEM jobs.

APPENDIX B
BIBLIOGRAPHY

About Pharmacy. Pharmacy College Application Service. N.d. Web. 7-17 Jul. 2016. www.pharmcas.org

Accelerating Science. CERN, European Council for Nuclear Research. N.d. Web. 7-17 Jul. 2016. https://home.cern/

Aczel, Amir D. *Chance: A Guide to Gambling, Love, the Stock Market, and Just About Everything Else.* New York: Thunder's Mouth Press, 2004.

"America's Pressing Challenge—Building a Stronger Foundation." A Companion to Science and Engineering Indicators 2006. National Science Board, Feb. 2006. Web. 27 Jan. 2015. www.nsf.gov/news/news_summ.jsp?cntn_id=105859

Barnes, A. Harrison. "The Role of a Geospatial Analyst." The Smarter, Simpler CRM, 13 Feb. 2009. Web. 8 Jul. 2016. http://EzineArticles.com/1990005

Birch, Hayley, Mun Keat Looi, Colin Stuart. *The Big Questions in Science: The Quest to Solve the Great Unknowns.* London: André Deutsch, 2013.

Borzo, Gene. "Scholars and Scientists Explore Factors Underlying Serendipitous Discoveries." UChicago News. The University of Chicago, Jun. 2014. Web. 16 Jan. 2015. https://news.uchicago.edu/article/2014/06/19/scholars-and-scientists-explore-factors-underlying-serendipitous-discoveries

Cardona, Maria. "Why the National STEM Education Fund Is So Important." HuffPost Tech, Jul. 2013. Web. 11 Feb. 2015. www.huffingtonpost.com/maria-cardona/why-national-stem-education-fund-is-so-important_b_3314124.html

Career Opportunities. Penn State, Department of Astronomy & Astrophysics. N.d. Web. 7-17 Jul. 2016. http://astro.psu.edu/academics/undergraduate-studies/career-opportunities

Career Resources for K-12 Students & Parents. AIChE: The Global Home of Chemical Engineers. N.d. Web. 7-17 Jul. 2016. www.aiche.org/community/students/career-resources-k-12-students-parents

"Career Spotlight: Robotics Technician." Chegg. N.d. Web. 9 Jul. 2016. www.chegg.com/career-center/explore/robotics-technician

Careers. Society of Toxicology. N.d. Web. 7-17 Jul. 2016. www.toxicology.org/careers/

Careers in Botany. Botanical Society of America. N.d. Web. 7-17 Jul. 2016. http://cms.botany.org/home/careers-jobs/careers-in-botany.html

Careers in Human Genetics. The American Society of Human Genetics. N.d. Web. 7-17 Jul. 2016. www.ashg.org/education/careers.shtml

Careers in Microbiology. University of Georgia. N.d. Web. 7-17 Jul. 2016. http://mib.uga.edu/careers-microbiology

"Careers in Robotics: Job Options and Employment Outlook." Robotics Business Review, 15 Dec. 14. Web. 8 Jul. 2016. roboticsbusinessreview.com/careers_in_robotics_job_options_and_employment_outlook/

Carradice, Phil. "Robert Recorde—The Man Who Invented the Equals Sign." BBC Wales, Jun. 2010. Web. 18 Jan. 2015. www.bbc.co.uk/blogs/wales/posts/robert_recorde

Cherry, Kendra. "Introduction to Research Methods." About Education. N.d. Web. 23 Jan. 2015. www.psychology.about.com/od/researchmethods/ss/expdesintro_2.htm

College of Engineering, Civil Engineering. University of Arkansas. N.d. Web. 7-10 Jul. 2016. http://civil-engineering.uark.edu/

College of Engineering, Electrical Engineering. University of Arkansas. N.d. Web. 7-10 Jul. 2016. http://electrical-engineering.uark.edu/

College to Career. America Chemical Society. N.d. Web. 7-17 Jul. 2016. https://www.acs.org/content/acs/en/careers/college-to-career .html

Condensed Matter Physics & Materials Science. Brookhaven National Laboratory. N.d. Web. 7-17 Jul. 2016. https://www.bnl.gov/ cmpmsd/

Coolmath. Coolmath.com LLC. N.d. Web. 8 Jan. 2015. www.coolmath.com

DeAngelis, Stephen F. "STEM Education: Why It's Important." Enterra Solutions, Mar. 2014. Web. 12 Feb. 2015. www .enterrasolutions.com/2014/03/stem-education-important.html

Department of Physics. Stanford University. N.d. Web. 7-17 Jul. 2016. https://physics.stanford.edu/

Dickens, Donna. "27 Science Fictions That Became Science Facts in 2012." BuzzFeed News, Dec. 2012. Web. 22 Jan. 2015. www.buzzfeed .com/donnad/27-science-fictions-that-became-science-facts-in-2

Divisions. Blogs of the European Geosciences Union. N.d. Web. 7-17 Jul. 2016. http://blogs.egu.eu/divisions/

Douglass, Charlene. "Euclid." Math Open Reference, 2007. Web. 12 Jan. 2015. www.mathopenref.com/euclid.html

Douglass, Charlene. "Pythagoras." Math Open Reference, 2005. Web. 14 Jan. 2015. www.mathopenref.com/pythagoras.html

"Drops on a Penny." Online Science Resources. Science World at Telus World of Science. N.d. Web. 23 Jan. 2015. www.scienceworld .ca/resources/activities/drops-penny

Dunn, Katie. "Why Is STEM Important in K–12 Education?" Daily Genius, 23 Oct. 2014. Web. 12 Jan. 2015. www.dailygenius.com/ stem-important-k-12-education/

Eberle, Francis. "Why STEM Education Is Important." *InTech Magazine*. ISA Publications, Sept. 2010. Web. 27 Jan. 2015. www.isa.org/standards-and-publications/ isa-publications/intech-magazine/2010/september/ why-stem-education-is-important/

Ecosystem Science and Management. University of Wyoming. N.d. Web. 7-17 Jul. 2016. www.uwyo.edu/esm

EducatingEngineers.com. N.d. Web. 7-17 Jul. 2016. www.educatingengineers.com

Education & Careers. American Meteorological Society. N.d. Web. 7-17 Jul. 2016. www.ametsoc.org/ams/index.cfm/education-careers/

Education & Public Engagement. National Optical Astronomy Observatory. N.d. Web. 7-17 Jul. 2016. www.noao.edu/education/

Education. Biophysical Society. N.d. Web. 7-17 Jul. 2016. www.biophysics.org/Education/WhatisBiophysics/tabid/2287/Default.aspx

Education. Seismological Society of America. N.d. Web. 7-17 Jul. 2016. www.seismosoc.org/inside/education/

"Elementary Science Experiments: Penny Drops." Kids-Fun-Science.com. Ring of Fire Science Company. N.d. Web. 24 Jan. 2015. www.kids-fun-science.com/elementary-science-experiments.html

"Etymology of the Term Dollar." The Titi Tudorancea Bulletin, Jun. 2008. Web. 24 Jan. 2015. www.tititudorancea.com/z/etymology_of_the_term_dollar.htm

"Euclid." Famous Scientists. N.d. Web. 12 Jan. 2015. www.famousscientists.org/euclid

Evans, Barry. "Serendipity in Science." North Coast Journal, Aug. 2010. Web. 16 Jan. 2015. www.northcoastjournal.com/humboldt/serendipity-in-science/Content?oid=2131243

"Forget Algebra—Is Statistics Necessary?" Statistics Learning Centre, 6 Aug. 2012. Web. 16 Jan. 2015. www.learnandteachstatistics.wordpress.com/2012/08/06/stats-not-algebra/

Hale, Jamie. "Understanding Research Methodology 5: Applied and Basic Research." World of Psychology. Psych Central. N.d. Web. 23 Jan. 2015. www.psychcentral.com/blog/archives/2011/05/12/understanding-research-methodology-5-applied-and-basic-research/

Helmenstine, Anne Marie. "Scientific Method Steps." About Education. N.d. Web. 16 Jan. 2015. www.chemistry.about.com/od/lecturenotesl3/a/sciencemethod.htm

"Hexadecimal Numbering System." Electronics Tutorials. Basic Electronics Tutorials by Wayne Storr. N.d. Web. 29 Jan. 2015. www.electronics-tutorials.ws/binary/bin_3.html

Hom, Elaine J. "What Is STEM Education?" LiveScience, Feb. 2014. Web. 27 Jan. 2015. www.livescience.com/43296-what-is-stem-education.html

"How Many Drops?" TeachEngineering. N.d. Web. 23 Jan. 2015. www.teachengineering.org/lessons/view/duk_drops_mary_less

"How to Become a Cryptologist—Career Guide & Jobs." Academic Invest. N.d. Web. 7 Jul. 2016. www.academicinvest
.com/science-careers/computer-science-careers/
how-to-become-a-cryptologist

"How to Become a Web Developer." ComputerScienceMajor.org. N.d. Web. 7 Jul. 2016. www.computersciencemajor.org/web-developer/

Huffman, Carl. "Pythagoras." The Stanford Encyclopedia of Philosophy (Summer 2014 edition), Edward N. Zalta (ed.), The Metaphysics Research Lab, Center for the Study of Language and Information. N.d. Web. 14 Jan. 2015. http://plato.stanford.edu/
entries/pythagoras

"Hun Dred No Longer." Membean. N.d. Web. 1 Feb. 2015. www.membean.com/wrotds/cent-hundred

Imagine the Universe! National Aeronautics and Space Administration. N.d. Web. 7-17 Jul. 2016. http://imagine.gsfc.nasa
.gov/

Jahn, Jody L.S., and Karen K. Myers. "Vocational Anticipatory Socialization of Adolescents: Messages, Sources, and Frameworks That Influence Interest in STEM Careers." Journal of Applied Communication Research, Vol. 42 (2014): 85–106.

"Job Outlook for: Mathematicians." CareerPlanner.com. N.d. Web. 7 Jul. 2016. http://job-outlook.careerplanner.com/Mathematicians
.cfm

Job Profiles. National Career Services. N.d. Web. 7-17 Jul. 2016. https://nationalcareersservice.direct.gov.uk/

Jobs. Physics Today. N.d. Web. 7-17 Jul. 2016. http://jobs.physics
today.org

Kelly, Brian. "The State of STEM and Jobs." U.S. News & World Report, Sept. 2012. Web. 28 Jan. 2015. www.usnews.com/news/articles/2012/09/21/the-state-of-stem-and-jobs

Kurtz, Annalyn. "The Best Job You Never Thought Of." CNN Money, 25 Apr. 2013. Web. 7 Jul. 2016. http://money.cnn.com/2013/04/25/news/economy/best-job-actuary/

"Large Number." MathWorld. Wolfram. N.d. Web. 28 Jan. 2015. www.mathworld.wolfram.com/LargeNumber.html

Lev-Ram, Michal. "The Business Case for STEM Education." *Fortune*, Jan. 2015. Web. 10 Feb. 2015. www.fortune.com/2015/01/22/the-business-case-for-stem-education/

Lind, Douglas A., William G. Marchal, and Samuel A. Wathen. *Statistical Techniques in Business & Economics, 15th Edition*. New York: McGraw-Hill, 2012.

Maston, John. "The Origin of Zero." *Scientific American*, Aug. 2009. Web. 22 Jan. 2015. www.scientificamerican.com/article/history-of-zero/

McKay, Dawn Rosenburg. "Market Research Analyst." The Balance, 29 Jan. 2015. Web. 7 Jul. 2016. www.thebalance.com/market-research-analyst-526044

Mechanical Engineering. Columbia Engineering. N.d. Web. 7-10 Jul. 2016. http://me.columbia.edu/

"More Than a Million." FactMonster. Family Education Network, Pearson Education. N.d. Web. 28 Jan. 2015. www.factmonster.com/ipka/A0769538.html

Morella, Michael. "Many High Schoolers Giving Up on STEM." U.S. News & World Report, Jan. 2013. Web. 29 Jan. 2015. www.usnews.com/news/blogs/stem-education/2013/01/31/report-many-high-schoolers-giving-up-on-stem

Morgan, Tracy. "The Importance of Extracurricular STEM Education." TeenLife Blog, Jan. 2015. Web. 29 Jan. 2015. www.teenlife.com/blogs/articles/the-importance-of-extra-curricular-stem-learning

Nagel, David. "'Job Shadowing' Can Get Students More Interested in STEM Careers." *The Journal*, Feb. 2014. Web. 27 Jan. 2015. http://thejournal.com/articles/2014/02/13/job-shadowing-can-get-students-more-interested-in-stem-careers.aspx

Natural Hazards. Natural Resources Canada. N.d. Web. 7-17 Jul. 2016. www.nrcan.gc.ca/hazards/natural-hazards

New Civil Engineer. N.d. Web. 7-10 Jul. 2016. http://newcivilengineer.info/

Newitz, Annalee. "One of the World's First Statements about the Scientific Method." Io9, Apr. 2014. Web. 22 Jan. 2015. www.io9.com/one-of-the-worlds-first-statements-about-the-scientific-1564545837

NSSL People. The National Severe Storms Laboratory. N.d. Web. 7-17 Jul. 2016. www.nssl.noaa.gov/people/jobs/

"Occupational Outlook: Financial Analysts and Advisors." AccountingJobsToday.com. N.d. Web. 7 Jul. 2016. www.accountingjobstoday.com/cm/Articles/occupational-outlook-financial-analyst.html

Occupational Outlook Handbook. Bureau of Labor Statistics. N.d. Web. 7-17 Jul. 2016. www.bls.gov/ooh/

Oladipo, Jennifer. "Students Branch Out with STEM Job Shadowing." *Upstate Business Journal*, Aug. 2013. Web. 27 Jan. 2015. http://upstatebusinessjournal.com/news/students-branch-out-with-stem-job-shadowing

"On-Time Arrival Performance, National (June, 2016)."Airline On-Time Statistics and Delay Causes. Bureau of Transportation Studies. N.d. Web. 17 Aug. 2016. www.transtats.bts.gov/OT_Delay/OT_DelayCause1.asp

Parker, Mike. "What Is the Job Outlook for Teachers?" *Houston Chronicle*. N.d. Web. 7 Jul. 2016. http://work.chron.com/job-outlook-teachers-12360.html

"Protractors." National Museum of American History. Smithsonian. N.d. Web. 17 Jan. 2015. www.americanhistory.si.edu/collections/object-groups/protractors

"Real-Time Insight Into the Market for Entry-Level STEM Jobs." Burning Glass Careers in Focus. Burning Glass Technologies, Feb. 2014. Web. 27 Jan. 2015. www.burning-glass.com/research/stem/

Schraml, Todd. "Defining the Role of the Data Architect." Database Trends and Applications. 11 Dec. 2012. Web. 8 Jul. 2016. www.dbta .com/Editorial/Think-About-It/Defining-the-Role-of-the-Data-Architect-86586.aspx

"Science At Multiple Levels." Understanding Science. University of California Museum of Paleontology. N.d. Web. 24 Jan. 2015. http:// undsci.berkeley.edu/article/howscienceworks_19

Science Buddies Staff. "Measuring Surface Tension of Water with a Penny." Science Buddies, Oct. 2014. Web. 23 Jan. 2015. www.sciencebuddies.org/science-fair-projects/project_ideas/ Chem_p021.shtml

"Science Fiction or Science Fact?" NASA. N.d. Web. 22 Jan. 2015. www.nasa.gov/multimedia/mmgallery/fact_fiction_nonflash_prt .htm

"Science Teacher Career Guide." N.d. Web. 7 Jul. 2016. www .teachercertificationdegrees.com/careers/science-teacher/

Smith, Kelli. "41 Jobs Titles in Tech: Which One Will Be Yours?" Skillcrush. 5 Mar. 2015. Web. 8 Jul. 2016. https://skillcrush .com/2015/03/05/41-tech-job-titles

Southwest Fisheries Science Center. National Oceanic and Atmospheric Administration. N.d. Web. 7-17 Jul. 2016. https://swfsc .noaa.gov/

"Statistician (Statistics) Careers, Jobs, and Education Information." Career Overview. N.d. Web. 7 Jul. 2016. www.careeroverview.com/ statistician-careers.html

"Steps of the Scientific Method." Science Buddies. N.d. Web. 14 Jan. 2015. www.sciencebuddies.org/science-fair-projects/project_ scientific_method.shtml

"Taxonomy of Fields and Their Subfields." National Academy of Sciences. Jul. 2006. Web. 15 Jan. 2015. http://sites .nationalacademies.org/PGA/Resdoc/PGA_044522

"The Future of U.S. Manufacturing and the Importance of STEM Education." Mid-Atlantic Technology, Research & Innovation Center. N.d. Web. 29 Jan. 2015. www.matricinnovates.com/education/the-future-of-u-s-manufacturing-and-the-importance-of-stem-education/

The USGS Water Science School. U.S. Geological Survey. N.d. Web. 7-17 Jul. 2016. http://water.usgs.gov/edu/

"Understanding and Using the Scientific Method." Science Made Simple. N.d. Web. 21 Jan. 2015. www.sciencemadesimple.com/scientific_method.html

"Understanding the Birthday Paradox." Better Explained. N.d. Web. 29 Jan. 2015. www.betterexplained.com/articles/understanding-the-birthday-paradox/

Wallin, Nils-Bertil. "The History of Zero: How Was Zero Discovered?" YaleGlobal Online. MacMillan Center, Nov. 2002. Web. 22 Jan. 2015. www.yaleglobal.yale.edu/about/zero.jsp

Watkins, Denny. "10 Medical Breakthroughs That Sound Like Science Fiction." Men's Health, Nov. 2014. Web. 22 Jan. 2014. www.menshealth.com/health/medical-breakthroughs

Weisstein, Eric W. "René Descartes (1596 – 1650)." Eric Weisstein's World of Scientific Biography. Wolfram Research. N.d. Web. 20 Jan. 2015. http://scienceworld.wolfram.com/biography/Descartes.html

WeUseMath.org. N.d. Web. 7-17 Jul. 2016. www.weusemath.org

"Why STEM Education Is Important for Everyone." Science Pioneers. N.d. Web. 27 Jan. 2015. www.sciencepioneers.org/parents/why-stem-is-important-to-everyone

"Your Next Job: Mobile App Developer? Computerworld. N.d. Web. 7 Jul. 2016. www.computerworld.com/article/2509463/app-development/your-next-job--mobile-app-developer-.html

INDEX

Abscissa, 189
Acceleration, 121–24
Accountant, 220
Acidic activity, 135–38
Action/reaction activity, 73–76
Actuary, 196
Aerospace engineer, 65
Air resistance, 122–24
Algebra activity, 179–82
Alkaline activity, 135–38
Analytical chemist, 134
Area of circle, 185–86
Area of triangle, 68
Astronomer, 95
Astronomy activities, 90–102
Astrophysicist, 99
Atoms, 45, 75, 79–80, 111, 133–35, 144
Automotive engineer, 63
Averages, calculating, 193–98, 201

Balloon force activity, 73–75
Balloon-powered car, 52–54
Bar chart activity, 203–6
Batteries activity, 130–34
Behavioral sciences, 14
Biochemist, 138
Biologists, 157, 161–62
Biology, 11, 149
Biology activities, 149–70
Biophysicist, 102
Biotechnologist, 162
Birthday problem activity, 216–17
Boat, soap-powered, 55–57

Botanist, 152
Bowling ball activity, 76–78
Bridge, building, 33–36
Building activities, 23–40, 45
Buoyancy, 113–19

Car, balloon-powered, 52–54
Car race, 58–63
Careers, 7–8, 11–14, 241–43. See also specific careers
Cartesian coordinate system, 187
Cartesian plane, 186
Cartesian treasure map activity, 186–89
Cell osmosis activity, 163–67
Charts/graphs activity, 199–206
Chemical engineer, 132
Chemistry, 12
Chemistry activities, 129–48
Chemists, 134, 138, 142, 145, 148
Chlorophyll, 152
Chord, 183
Circuits, building, 37–40, 45
Circumference activity, 183–85
Civil engineer, 32
Cold/warm activity, 110–12
Complement rule, 210
Computer programmer, 175, 178, 226, 230, 235
Computer sciences, 13
Computer sciences activities, 171–226
Computer systems analyst, 178
Condensed-matter physicist, 78
Conductor activity, 41–46

Constellations, recognizing, 100–102
Coordinate system activity, 186–89
Cryptographer, 208
Curie temperature, 86

Data architect, 180
Database administrator, 185
Deciduous trees, 154–58
Decimals, 173, 177, 218–24
Density activity, 113–19
Diameter activity, 183–85
Dry ice activity, 146–48

Earth sciences, 12
Earth sciences activities, 103–27
Ecologist, 153
Economist, 217
Electric circuits, building, 37–40, 45
Electrical engineer, 46
Electricity activity, 47–51
Electricity, static, 40, 79–83
Electrolytes, 45–46, 131–34
Electromagnets, 51
Electronegativity, 133
Electrons, 39–40, 78–83, 132–35
Elements, periodic table of, 126–27, 144
Engineering, 13–14
Engineering activities, 23–68
Engineers, 32, 46, 51, 63, 65, 68, 132, 156, 226, 229
Enrichment classes, 228–33
Environmental engineers, 156
Environmental scientists, 156
Euclidean geometry, 190
Evaporation, 144, 147–48
Evergreen trees, 154–58
Experimentation, 10
Exponents, 177

Faraday cage, 81
Feather activity, 120–24
Fermentation activity, 159–62
Ferromagnetic material, 88–89

Financial analyst, 225
Floating/sinking activities, 113–19
Force of gravity activities, 70–78, 120–24
Force pairs law, 73–75
Fractions, 173–74, 176
Frozen/liquid activities, 70–72, 146–48

Genetic traits activity, 168–70
Geneticist, 170
Genetics, father of, 169
Geographic poles activity, 104–9
Geologists, 109
Geometry, father of, 190
Geometry scavenger hunt activity, 190–92
Geospatial analyst, 188
Googol, 218
Graphs/charts activity, 199–206
Gravity activities, 70–78, 120–24
Grid activity, 172–74

Hereditary traits activity, 168–70
Hydrologist, 115
Hypothesis, 15–17

Ice activity, 146–48
Industrial engineer, 68
Inertia, law of, 70, 77–78
Insulator activity, 41–46
Interest, calculating, 222–26
Ions, 45, 132–36, 144

Job shadowing, 236–39
Juice cans, racing, 70–72

Lab technician, 148
Learning resources, 228–36
Life sciences, 11, 149. See also Biology activities
Liquid/frozen activities, 70–72, 146–48

Magnetic field, 49–50, 89
Magnetic materials, 87–89

Magnetic poles activity, 104–9
Magnetism activities, 47–51,
  84–89, 104–9
Map activity, 186–89
Marine biologist, 157
Market research analyst, 203
Mass, 78, 116–19, 121
Math review activity, 175–78
Mathematician, 174
Mathematics, 11, 13
Mathematics activities, 171–226
Matter, 11–12, 70–71, 78–80,
  116–18
Mechanical engineer, 51
Meteorologist, 112
Microbiologist, 157, 161
Mobile app developer, 230
Molecules, 55, 57, 80, 110–12
Momentum, 121–24
Money value activities, 222–26
Moon phase journal, 90–92
Moon-phase navigation, 93–99
Motor, building, 24–27
Mousetrap car race, 58–63
Mutually exclusive categories,
  202–3, 209–10

Nanotechnology, 12, 45
Neutrons, 80
Newton's cradle, 75
Newton's laws of motion, 70–77,
  121, 124
North pole activity, 104–9
Nuclear physicist, 75

Oceanographer, 127
Order of operations, 178
Ordinate, 189
Organisms, 102, 126–27, 149–53,
  159–62
Osmosis activity, 163–67

Particle physicist, 79
Particles, 75, 79–80
Percentages activity, 172–74
Periodic table of elements,
  126–27, 144

Permanent magnet, 87–89
PH activity, 136–42
Pharmacologist, 142
Photosynthesis activity, 150–53
Physical science, 11–12
Physicists, 70, 75, 78–79, 86, 99,
  102
Physics, 12, 69–70
Physics activities, 69–89
Physics, father of, 70
Pi, 184–85
Pictograph, 206
Pie chart activity, 199–203
Place value activity, 218–24
Plant scientists, 152
Plants activity, 150–58
Pressure activity, 110–12
Probability activity, 207–15
Probability, classical, 207
Probability, empirical, 212
Probability range, 209
Protons, 79–83, 135
Pyramids activity, 66–68
Pythagorean theorem, 67–68

Racing cars, 58–63
Racing juice cans, 70–72
Radius activity, 183–85
Range, calculating, 195
Raw data, 200–202
Resources, 228–36, 241–43
Robotics engineer, 229
Robotics technician, 229
Rocket launch, 64–65

Salt-separation activity, 143–45
Science. See also STEM
  careers in, 7–8, 11–14, 241–43
  explanation of, 10–11
  fields in, 7–8, 11–14, 236–39
  types of, 11–14
Science fact activity, 20–21
Science fiction activity, 20–21
Science teacher, 11
Science writer, 13
Scientific method activity, 14–19
Scientists, 126, 152, 156

Seismologist, 123
Semipermeable surface, 163–66
Serendipity, 10
Sinking/floating activities,
    113–19
Soap-powered boat, 55–57
Social sciences, 14
Software engineer, 226
Soil composition activity, 125–27
Soil scientist, 126
Solutes, 164–67
Solvents, 164–66
South pole activity, 104–9
Static electricity, 40, 83
Static electricity activity, 79–83
Statistician, 193, 196, 198
STEM
    basics of, 9–17
    camps for, 228–31
    careers in, 7–8, 11–14, 241–43
    classes for, 228–33
    explanation of, 7–8
    fields in, 7–8, 11–14, 236–39
    groups for, 228–31
    head start in, 227–39
    job shadowing in, 236–39
    resources for, 228–36, 241–43

Sublimation, 147–48
Surface tension, 55–57

Temperatures, 86, 110–12
Theoretical physicists, 70, 79
Tic-tac-toe math activity, 175–78
Toxicologist, 145
Trees activity, 154–58
Triangles activity, 66–68
Trusses, building, 28–32

Velocity, 76–77, 122
Velocity activities, 76–78, 120–24
Volume, 116–19

Warm/cold activity, 110–12
Water activities, 55–57, 113–19
Water rocket launch, 64–65
Weather activities, 110–12
Web developer, 235
Zeros in quadrillion activity,
    218–21
Zoologist, 166